I0415111

GENERATION
BUSTED

How America Went Broke in the
Age of Prosperity

©Alan J. Zemek 2010

Copyright 2010 Alan J Zemek
Laguna Niguel, California 92677
ISBN 978-1-451-51686-9

Cover photography: Ozgur Donma
Printed in the United States of America

www.generationbusted.com

For Keiko,
Who makes all things possible

Special Thanks to:
Dr. Karl Egge, Chairman of the Department of Economics
Macalester College, Saint Paul Minnesota

CONTENTS

Table of Illustrations

Preface

"Never Trust Anyone over the Age of Thirty"

If you are a baby boomer, you might have a vague recollection of this phrase. Our generation championed this expression in the 1960's to give voice to both our distrust of the establishment and our aspirations for change. Our sheer numbers and influence shaped the course of politics and the economy for the next sixty years, and brought with it a whirlwind of new social thinking. But that was nothing like the hurricane that is about to come over the horizon today. We don't have a National Weather Service warning for demographic change, but there are some ominous economic storm clouds out there, and they are worthy of some close attention...

It is now 2011, and the first wave of baby boomers to reach the traditional retirement milestone age of 65 is out there, waiting to retire, start drawing their social security checks and rely upon Medicare for their healthcare. This generation will consume more public resources than any generation in history, and most will glibly maintain their sense of entitlement to do it, regardless of the consequences to the rest of us.

The year 2011 will mark the beginning of a long wave demographic earthquake on a tectonic scale. The demand for government funded services is about to explode beyond anything we are familiar with today. As more and more retiring baby boomers demand an unprecedented level of government services they believe they are entitled to receive, the heavier will become the tax burden on the productive classes of our society, the young, the ambitious, the creative, and the inventive.

This burden is about to fall upon the unsuspecting children of the baby boomers, just as policy makers are simultaneously attempting to prove the tenuous hypothesis that a higher standard of living can be attained by making energy less available and more expensive. I believe very few of them appreciate just how recently the age of prosperity came upon us, and how tenuously we are holding on to it.

This book is meant for surfing. There are more complete books out there that explain the economics. There are plenty of learned historical treatises that go into much more depth. There are better first person accounts of the financial melt down of 2008, and how unregulated risk traders nearly imploded the financial system of the entire planet, so I make no claim to any original idea or thesis, other than my own opinions, when I state them.

But I do think this book will be particularly valuable to the younger audience, for whom the policies and politics of the last sixty years might as well be ancient history. Much of the story is worthy of rejoicing. The baby boomers' idealism and hope transformed a fearful and segregated society, opened opportunities for women and minorities, advanced social tolerance and the dignity of working people everywhere, and laid the foundation for the survival of the planet.

But it is also the story of an exaggerated sense of entitlement, irresponsible behavior, and vastly unrealistic expectations of instant gratification. It is the great contradiction of our age. The tremendous social progress of the last sixty years was only made possible by an incredibly productive private enterprise system that created the modern age of prosperity as we know it. Somewhere along the way, many social thinkers took our prosperity for granted, and for many, prosperity itself became the ultimate entitlement.

Here is one fundamental truth we should never take for granted: social progress is made because of the wealth creating potential of the private enterprise economy, not in spite of it. This is the fundamental organizing idea that created the modern world.

And finally, for you baby boomers out there, if you are one of us, you had better hide this book from your children. Because when they discover the legacy we have left for them, they just might pick up where we left off fifty years ago, and decide to take our own advice:

-"Never Trust Anyone over the Age of Thirty"

✧✧✧ **INTRODUCTION** ✧✧✧

✧✧✧

Congratulations, You Are Broke

America is headed for bankruptcy.   This is not exaggeration, hyperbole, or alarmism. It is a true statement of a statistical fact. The definition of bankruptcy is a legally declared inability of a debtor to meet its obligations to its creditors. If you were born after 1980, congratulations, you belong to Generation Busted.

In the 1960's your parents, or maybe your grandparents, liked to use the phrase "Never trust anyone over the age of thirty". If you belong to Generation Busted, it might be time to revive that distrust and suspicion of the economic and political establishment, because the generation gap that existed then is nothing compared to the generation gap that is looming ahead for you. Your parents and grandparents bankrupted you, and you don't even know it yet. I wrote this book for you, so you will know how and why it happened.

If you think I am exaggerating, consider this: gross public debt in this country peaked at more than 128% of gross domestic product in 1946, reflecting the staggering cost of defeating Germany, Italy, and Japan, at the end of World War Two. For the next 35 years, until 1981, gross public debt as percentage of gross domestic product declined, almost without exception, every single year. The debt burden on the economy was slashed by three fourths, from 128% of GDP, down to 32%, which is about where it was in 1931. It had taken 35 years to pay down the debts left over from a decade of chaos, economic depression, global war, and finally, economic recovery. 1981 was the last year the debt load on the economy saw any meaningful decline.

In fact, in the 35 years since 1981, the debt load on the economy is again expected to hit 128% of gross domestic product, right back where it was in 1946. And you won't even get a victory parade.

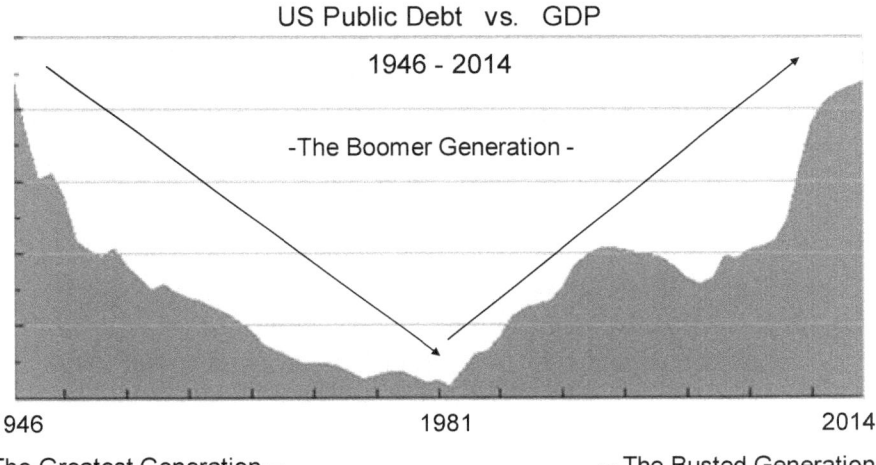

GENERATION BUSTED
US Public Debt   vs.   GDP
1946 - 2014

-The Boomer Generation -

1946   1981   2014

The Greatest Generation –   – The Busted Generation

Source: www.usgovernmentspending.com

In 1946 we were the Greatest Generation; in 1964 we were the Boomer Generation, and if you were born after 1981, well, welcome to the Busted Generation. America is broke, and the burden of paying off America's debts is going to fall on your shoulders.

This book is about debt. What it is, where it came from, how it functions, and what it means for your future. Debt is like gravity. It is an irresistible force. There is no escaping it once it has sucked you in, but great empires and epic fortunes can be, and have been built upon it. Debt is nothing more than a tool. It can be used artfully or clumsily, just like any other. In skillful hands, debt has an enormous creative power to generate vast wealth, lift standards of living, create prosperity and alleviate all manner of suffering and misery. Used poorly, it has literally precipitated world wars, social collapse, revolution, mass murder, and the disintegration of global empires.

This book is also about economics and markets, because debt is a commodity that is traded every day, just like bushels of wheat, barrels of oil, ounces of gold or gallons of orange juice. Once you understand what debt is and how it works, the next step is to understand how the price of debt is determined, who buys it, who sells it, and why.

Debt is also a state of mind. What you know about debt, how you feel about debt, and your attitude about debt in general probably determines more about your personal financial health and well being than anything else you know, feel or believe. So, what does it mean to be in debt?

Consider the following statement: Total U.S. federal debt is now about 14 trillion dollars[1]. In ten years it will be over 20 trillion dollars. If current trends continue, in fifty years the debt will be over 40 trillion dollars. If you are a young adult just entering the work force today, your household share will be about $480,000 by the time you are ready to retire. On second thought, don't make any plans. You won't be able to afford to retire.[2]

---

[1] This number includes only the debts that are "on the books". The liability of the US Government for future Social Security and Medicare payments now exceeds $107 Trillion Dollars. This is a truly catastrophic number, more than seven times the size of the entire US economy! (www.NCPA.org)

[2] David Walker, US Comptroller General 1998-2008, in sworn testimony before the Senate Homeland Security Committee, December 17, 2009.

The current level of public debt in this country is a number so incomprehensibly large that it has virtually no value as a piece of quantitative information. The only real meaning it has for most people is how they *feel* about it. For some, it makes their blood boil about wasteful government spending and corrupt politicians in bed with corporate big wigs. For some, it is more a symptom of the cultural degradation of the modern world, a failure of moral restraint and a reason to despair for the future of Western Civilization. For others it creates something more like a vague sense of unease that you can't quite describe. I mean, really, who can even conceive of numbers that huge? Just how big is 14 trillion dollars anyway?

Actually, the most intellectually honest reaction to that number should be *"So what?"* Without some way of putting this number in context, it is just too hard to count that high.

This book will explain the "So what" of debt, how we got here, and what it means for our future. If it scares you, calms you, enlightens you, or entertains you, I will have fulfilled my purpose. By the way, can I borrow some money? I'll pay you back later.
I promise!

✧✧✧

Deal or No Deal?

So just how deep in debt are we? What does $14 *Trillion* Dollars in U.S. federal debt really mean? It means you, you personally, along with every other man, woman, and child alive in America today owe roughly $47,000 Dollars for the privilege of being an American citizen. This is your personal share. You owe it. You are going to pay it. Your children are going to pay it. And then their children are going to pay it. It is an inescapable truth and fact of life. In fact, you, your children, and their children will be making payments on the debts of this country for the entire duration of their natural lives. In the interest of full disclosure the U.S. government should send out letters addressed to every new born baby in the country:

"Congratulations, and welcome to the party. Here's your bill. You owe us $47,000, so hurry up, grow up, and get to work. Have a nice day!"

Are you depressed yet? Don't be. Why? Because your share of the national debt that you inherited, either by accident of birth, or by choice as an immigrant to this country, has been absolutely the greatest bargain in the history of all human civilization. I say "has been" because it has been absolutely true. Well, at least up until today. (What happens tomorrow is open to debate, but that comes later in the book).

Don't believe me? Let's play "Deal or no Deal?" Just like the popular television show. I will make you an offer and you tell me which suitcase you would like to open.

Suitcase One

You have the option to be born into a mythical sub-Saharan country called Afristan, and come into the world 100% debt free. If you are lucky, you will get three or four years of basic education, after which you will earn a subsistence level income for the rest of your life as a semi-literate farmer or herder. You might live to the ripe old age of 38, if drought, famine, disease, or war doesn't kill you first. You will live 1000 miles from the nearest paved road, airport, seaport, or modern hospital, and just to keep things really exciting, every couple of years or so, the local tribal militia will stop by and steal anything you have managed to accumulate, especially your women and female children.

If you are unfortunate enough to be born female, your prospects are probably even bleaker. You'll be lucky if you learn to read at all. You won't ever own any property. In fact, you most likely will be considered to be property: Some one else's property. The male members of your family will decide with whom and when you enter marriage, or they may just sell you off for a profit if circumstances become desperate enough. In any case, you will probably never travel more than a few miles from your place of birth.

Suitcase Two

You have the option to be born into the United States, where you will inherit at your birth personal responsibility for paying off your share of a massive public debt. You will work your whole life paying it off, and probably never even make a dent in it. Then, when you die, your kids will start paying it too.

However, in exchange for taking up this life long burden, you will receive somewhere between 12 and 18 years of free, or nearly free, education. You will be vaccinated against a plethora of crippling diseases and deadly viruses. You will live largely free from civic strife and chaos, reside in comfortable surroundings your whole life, and quite blissfully take for granted most of the comforts of modern living. Flip a switch and the lights will come on. Flush a handle and waste will disappear. Turn a faucet, and clean potable water will flow like magic right into your home. In fact, clean water is so cheap and plentiful you will spray it all over the land around your house with reckless abandon. And you won't even notice most extremes of weather, because your house and place of business will be climate controlled. You will always have plenty of food, most likely, too much food.

You will live within a short drive, maybe an hour or two at the most, from a major airport where for the small price of a few hours of your labor, you can get on a well maintained aircraft and travel thousands of miles completely unhindered (except for the indignity of having to take your shoes off at the security checkpoint). You can arrive in an unfamiliar city with total confidence that you can walk freely down the street as a complete stranger, and have almost no reasonable fear of being molested or accosted, either by the local police or the local riffraff.

So, what's it going to be? Deal, or no deal? Maybe that massive public debt doesn't seem so bad any more. The fact is that debt is an essential, necessary component of a modern standard of living and a functioning civil society. Debt is like oxygen. Most of the time, you take it for granted. Choke it off, and after a very brief period of panic and terror, everything comes to a dead stop. Get too much of it one place, and it burns explosively in very dramatic fashion, consuming everything it touches.

Like fire, water, electricity, and any other fundamental element of nature, it can be managed and used for good, or it can be used to unleash devastation and destruction. It is all in how you use it. It has a unique alchemy all its own. Those who understand it and yield it skillfully use it to acquire great wealth and power. For others, it is an unexploded roadside bomb capable of inflicting permanent injury on the unwary or unsuspecting.

So the next time you hear some one say with indignant and righteous fury that the national debt exceeds $14 *trillion* dollars, as if the sky were falling, your response should be *"So what?"* Yes, America is broke, but *so what?* What comes after the *so what?* is where things start to get really interesting.

✧✧✧ **PART ONE** ✧✧✧

The Foundation of American Prosperity

What do borrowed money, market speculation, and the Constitution of the United States all have in common? They are all a reflection of a commitment to the idea that a forward looking society that embraces dynamic change will prosper. All of these are tangible expressions of human imagination and a vision for the future; that tomorrow will be a better day.

And, surprisingly enough, each of these things, the Constitution, borrowed money, and market speculation, is an essential cornerstone in the foundation of modern prosperity. None of these alone work as well to create wealth and social progress as do all three of them working together.

American prosperity was built upon this foundation. It is a great story.

✧✧✧

The Constitutional Economy

"The Congress shall have power to borrow money on the credit of the United States."

-Article I, Section 8-2, Constitution of the United States

Nothing is more fundamentally important to understanding the foundation of 200 years of American prosperity than an insightful understanding of the Constitution of the United States of America. The Constitution is the most concise, coherent and powerful manifesto of economic principles and free market theory ever put down on eight short pages of handwritten text. The Constitution is where the story of our prosperity begins, so it is where I will begin also.

Article I of the U.S. Constitution created the Congress. The very first power granted to Congress was the power to tax. The very next power granted to Congress was the power to borrow money. The grant of power to tax and borrow money appears in the constitution even before the creation of the executive and judicial branches of government. Tax and spend is the essence of government, and we have been arguing about it ever since. We should at least know what we are arguing about.

The U.S. Constitution is a stunning achievement of elegance and simplicity. It is only eight pages of hand written text, yet it created the complete framework of governance that made it possible for a few vulnerable outpost cities perched on the edge of a wilderness continent to ascend into the richest most powerful society humanity has every known. It created a democratic republic that achieved total world dominance as an unchallenged military super power, and produced an economic model for prosperity that crushed tyrannies and empires everywhere on the planet. It created an economic explosion in wealth making capacity that lasted for more than two hundred years. Nothing has produced more wealth, more opportunity, more freedom, and more dignity for the common man than the economic model embodied in the Constitution of the United States. Period.

What made the new American republic so astonishingly successful? Was it really just a few ideas scratched down on several sparse pages of text? American constitutional democracy as we know it is either a work of divine inspiration or it is the result of the most propitious series of accidental coincidences in the history of civilization. What ever you believe, when you consider all of the possible constructions and forms of government that could have emerged from the colonization of the American continent, the Constitution of the United States is still the greatest living legacy of the Common Era, and the world's greatest hope for the continuation of liberty and prosperity. It is also the most misunderstood and misconstrued document of the modern age. Much of what you think you know about the Constitution is probably wrong.

In these modern times of political correctness, the Constitution is taught to school children and law students as primarily a political or legal document, either in a political science class, history class, or constitutional law class. Unfortunately, most law students don't know what they are studying because most law professors don't know what they are teaching. The popular understanding and teaching of the U.S. Constitution for the last two generation of students has focused almost exclusively on the Bill of Rights and a few other amendments, which are essentially about restraints on government powers, and the fair and equal administration of justice. This is both appropriate and necessary for a student of the law, but it teaches nothing about the foundational language of governance and economic prosperity. This is an unfortunate legacy; because the true source of liberty and justice for all is embodied in the economic theory revealed in Article I, which precedes the amendments. By rights, constitutional law should be taught in an economics class, as much as in a law class.

Of course there are the Articles that create three equal and separate branches of government to divide government powers, but most of the document we know as our Constitution is in fact a detailed treatise on economic theory and principles. Embodied within its clauses are the most profound ideas of liberty and freedom that were best articulated not by the politicians and lawyers who drafted it, but by the great Economists of the age.[3]

How is this so? If you read carefully, The U.S. Constitution is actually the world's first modern free trade agreement. While the Articles create the structure of governance in the political sense, the real meat of the Constitution is deeply rooted in economic policy: the power to tax, the power to coin money, the power to regulate commerce, the power to build roads, and post offices, the power to standardize weights and measures, the power to grant monopoly patent rights on new inventions, the requirement of uniformity in the levy of customs taxes and tariffs, the unrestricted free flow of goods across state lines, the full faith and credit provisions, the protection of private contracts, the validity of pre-adoption debts against the United States, and the

---

[3] Adam Smith 1723-1790 is best known for his work as an Economist, and his 1776 work *The Wealth of Nations*, but his education and training was rooted in moral philosophy. Many of the great economic theorists were heavily influenced by theology, philosophy and religion. See Professor Mark Thoma's lectures, (Univ. of Oregon) available on YouTube: *History of Economic Thought* for an excellent discussion on the development of modern economic theory.

power to borrow money are specifically enumerated in a document that is only eight pages in length.

In such a concise document the significance of this level of detail can not be under estimated. These are fundamental economic principles embedded within the very foundation of the Republic. These economic policy choices: free trade, private property rights, limited taxation, incentives for the invention of new and more productive machines and technologies, and a commitment to open markets, are what spawned the American economic miracle that swept across the continent, and then the world, within the span of a single lifetime.

While the Bill of Rights and the other amendments that work to guarantee personal privacy and civil liberties is rightly celebrated, it is the body of the Constitution itself that reveals the organizing principles of the Republic. It is the essential framework of prosperity. This is Truth, but it is mostly under appreciated because the Constitution is no longer widely taught as a deliberate expression of economic theory. This is both unfortunate and yet completely understandable. Given the two hundred years of spilled blood and misery it took to establish broad social acceptance of civil rights for all our citizens, civil liberty is surely an appropriate emphasis to teach, but it does not tell the whole story.

Here is a surprise for you: Capitalism freed the slaves. Capitalism ended racial segregation in this country. It is generally not well understood that the US Supreme Court gave life to the Federal Civil Rights Act of 1964 in two landmark cases, *Heart of Atlanta Motel v. United States,* and *Katzenbach v. McClung.* It was not through the Bill of Rights, or through the 14th Amendment, as you might expect, but through the free trade provisions of the Constitution: Article I, Section 8, the power to regulate commerce among the States, which incidentally, appears right after the power to tax and the power to borrow money. [4]

The Supreme Court ruled in these cases that Congress had the power to prohibit racial discrimination in privately owned hotels and restaurants, and effectively end the unconscionable sin of segregation. But not because it was a denial of basic civil liberties, but because segregation laws had a negative effect on interstate commerce!

Today it is hard to comprehend *Plessey v Ferguson*, the 1896 Supreme Court decision that held segregation laws did not violate the 14th amendment. It took an act of Congress sixty eight years later to undo this terrible injustice, but it did so not as a guarantee of fundamental civil rights, but as a federal act to regulate interstate commerce. Where the Supreme Court failed in 1896, Congress prevailed in 1964. It was a stunning achievement in the advancement of freedom. Sometimes Congress actually does get it right.

You should be asking yourself, what makes congressional power to regulate commerce among the states a manifesto of free trade? Because the drafters originally intended to prevent individual states from erecting trade barriers to the free flow of goods and the unfettered development of commerce among the states, and did so by reserving regulation of interstate commerce to the federal government. This is not an implied theory. The language in the Constitution is explicit. [5]

The 14th Amendment embodies our aspirations as a people for equality and fair treatment for all, but it is the Commerce Clause that gives Congress the means to put meat

[4] Barron Jerome A. & Dienes Thomas C. (2005). Constitutional Law 6th Ed. p.80-81
[5] Article One, Section 9, Constitution of the United States

on the bone. In fact, in the modern interpretation of the Constitution, the Commerce Clause has become one of the most important sources of federal control over the economy. It has very nearly evolved into a source of general police powers, which were never expressly granted to the federal government, but that some argue are now essential to the orderly development of an integrated global economy and potentially the preservation of the planet itself. It is the essence of the great debate of our time. What will best secure our prosperity in the challenge of our times?

Consolidating a Continent on Borrowed Money

It is no accident that the first article of the Constitution grants Congress the power to tax and spend before the other two branches of government are even mentioned. After 11 years of war for independence the Confederation of States that made up the former English colonies on the edge of the North American continent were broke and exhausted. When the Constitution was finally ratified in 1791 all the government's war debts were consolidated into federal obligations of the new United States of America. Federal debt was more than one third the entire gross domestic product of the new nation.[6]

The American Continental Army and the struggle for independence had very nearly collapsed for lack of funding on more than one occasion during the eleven year struggle to throw off the British Crown. While at Valley Forge the Army went without pay or supplies for months. Several years later, in June of 1783, disgruntled soldiers marched on the Congress in session in Philadelphia to petition for their unpaid wages. Congress was forced to relocate to Princeton New Jersey to escape the mob.[7]

---

[6] www.usgovernmentspending.com
[7] Chernow, Ron. *Alexander Hamilton*. Penguin Books, (2004)p180

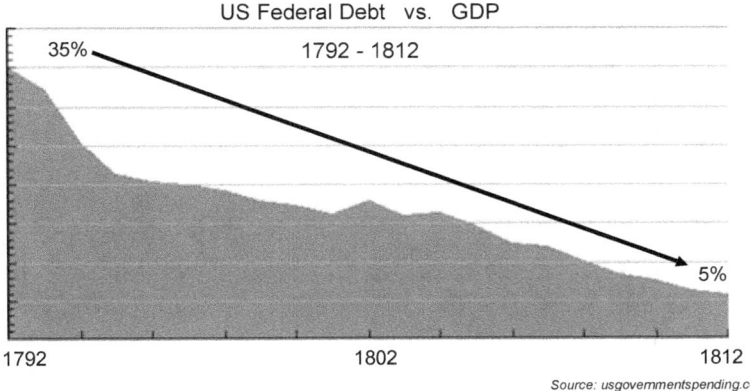

US Federal Debt vs. GDP
1792 - 1812

35%

5%

1792   1802   1812

Source: usgovernmentspending.com

Winning independence from England could easily have been a hollow victory. The hard won birth of the nation had left it near bankruptcy, and it could just as easily have reverted to tyranny or a new American monarchy. But for the next ten years, as the thirteen colonies became a large unified market operating with a single currency[8], the economy grew steadily and the federal debt as a share of gross domestic product was cut in half in a decade. The debt was simply absorbed into a new larger, more efficient and richer society. We had fought for our independence with blood and borrowed money, and carried the debt forward into the greater productive capacity of the new economy until it just disappeared. After a mere ten years of existence the new government of the United States was feeling bold enough to issue $11 million dollars in bonds to finance the Louisiana Purchase, the equivalent of about 2% of the gross domestic product of the economy at the time, and

---

[8] The National Currency Act that created the modern 'Greenback" as we know it was not passed until 1863, but the process of unified exchange was already underway.

with the stroke of a pen, doubled the size of the country. (Why conquer an empire when you can buy one?) The bond issue shows up as a small blip in an otherwise unbroken trend line of a declining debt burden on the economy.

Within the first twenty years of its history, this new nation, basically an untested social experiment, firmly rooted itself on the continent, doubled in size, and paid down its debt from 35% of the economy to a mere 5% of the economy. And as part of the deal the United States secured for itself the most contested and strategic city of the New World: The City of New Orleans.[9]

In some intellectual circles, capitalism is associated with oppression and slavery. This is a misplaced and dangerous conceit. In 1789 the new American nation rejected the European economic model of mercantile colonialism, and framed the nation's constitution in favor of the new economic science of democratic capitalism. But In 1792 when the Constitution was finally ratified, it still contained vestiges of the old world order. The contradiction of legal slavery remained unresolved as a political compromise so that the Constitution could be adopted by unanimous vote.

Seventy years later, what political compromise could not accomplish, the dynamism of capitalism did. The industrial productivity of the northern states combined with the capacity to finance huge government deficits became an insurmountable war fighting advantage for the Union.   By 1865 the Confederacy was utterly crushed under an avalanche of war production purchased with borrowed money. In the process, the United States government invented the key strategic weapon for a new kind of global super power: an almost unlimited reserve capacity for the government to surge the army on

---

[9] http://en.wikipedia.org/wiki/Louisiana_Purchase

borrowed money and to sustain massive deficits in times of national crisis. This capacity would be called upon again in the 20th century to defeat fascism, communism, rebuild a devastated world, and win a cold war that lasted more than forty years.

Colonial mercantilism had been the dominant economic model for more than 250 years, and it had created powerful economic interests that would not just quietly fade away. During the course of the 19th Century the United States expelled every great European power from the American continent, either by buying them out or pushing them out, including the acquisition of the Alaska territory from Imperial Russia in 1867, which turned out to be the greatest land deal of all time.[10]

The final punctuation mark was the battle of Manila Bay on May 1, 1898. Three hundred years of Spanish control of the Philippine Islands ended in a matter of hours when the US Asiatic fleet destroyed the Spanish fleet based there, and entered Manila Harbor at a cost of nine wounded sailors.[11] The entire Spanish American War of 1898 was over in about sixteen weeks. Hardly enough time to even issue a war bond.[12]

Wherever democratic capitalism and the dynamism of American Constitutionalism came into conflict with a competing economic system, capitalism prevailed with astonishing success. The history of federal government borrowing and intervention into the economy until well into the 20th Century was pretty much limited to financing deficits in

---

[10] http://www.loc.gov/rr/program/bib/ourdocs/Alaska.html
[11] The battle for the Philippines was something of a charade, to allow the Spanish a way to get out by handing the government over to the U.S., instead of Filipino insurgents. The U.S. Army conducted brutal counter insurgency operations from 1899 until 1913 to pacify the islands.
[12] http://www.state.gov/r/pa/ho/time/gp/90609.htm

time of war, and then letting a larger, more productive economy absorb the war debts through economic growth in the intervals between wars.

For good or for bad, in the 19th Century the United States government for the most part did not intervene in the economy, did not spend very much money on anything other than paying for national defense, taking opportunistic territorial gains at the suffering of indigenous peoples , and buying up the remnants of bankrupt colonial empires.

The commitment to an unfettered and unrestrained free market economic policy was so deeply and pervasively entrenched in the political thinking of the time that in 1905 the US Supreme Court in *Lochner v. New York* actually overturned a New York labor law limiting the work week of bakery employees to no more than ten hours per day and 60 hours per week. The court reasoned that the regulation was an unconstitutional regulation of private economic rights, and an unreasonable intrusion into the personal liberty to form private contracts for the purchase or sale of individual labor. The year 1905 was the high-water mark for rawest form of pure capitalism in the United States. [13]

This doctrine of Economic Due Process Rights was quickly abandoned by the court as it soon recognized that State laws for the regulation of health and general welfare were, quite correctly, police powers within the prerogative of the legislative branch of government as legitimate policy choices and worthy of judicial deference. Even so, it would take another thirty years and the near meltdown of the economy before it became generally acceptable for the government to even entertain the idea of actively formulating economic policy

---

[13]Barron Jerome A. & Dienes Thomas C. (2005). Constitutional Law 6th Ed. p.193-197

for intervention in the economy when the country was not at war.

The Constitutional blueprint for an economic model based on free trade, secure property rights, limited taxation and little intervention in the economy by the government had worked fabulously for more than a century. But by the late 19th century there was a growing social movement and legitimate concern that the wealth concentrating power of capitalism might overwhelm the very democratic institutions that gave birth to the nation's vast riches. There was no question that the free market economy could produce enormous wealth. But could it make things *fair?*[14]This is a completely different concept than what is *just*.

The Constitution of the United States actually has very little to say about "fairness" as an economic policy objective of the government. The text of the Constitution is actually quite bland. Congress makes the rules, the Executive carries them out, and any disagreements get adjudicated in the Supreme Court. The rest of it is mostly a rather dry and not-so inspiring rendition of economic theory that most political science students would rather skip right over. The Bill of Rights is just a lot sexier. Economic doctrine is pretty dull compared to our most celebrated aspirations for individual liberties and civil rights, which are all found somewhere else; In the Declaration of Independence, the Bill of Rights, The Gettysburg Address, and the great inaugural speeches of our most inspired Presidents.

We should certainly celebrate the extraordinary achievements of those who suffered to advance the cause of freedom, but we should also appreciate the Constitution for what it is: A model of practicality, a deliberate expression of a

---

[14] http://www.nps.gov/archive/elro/glossary/progressive-era.htm

model of limited government based on secure property rights and free markets to secure the greater prosperity of the nation. The Constitution picks no winners, and makes no statements about what is *"fair."* The Constitution is about *justice*, not *fairness.*

Every first year student of Economics will encounter the concept of "fairness" as the difference between positive and normative economics. Positive economics is an objective description of how things are, in theory and behavior. Normative economics is a subjective description of how things "should be." "Healthcare should be free" is a subjective value statement. "If Medicare reimbursement for primary doctors is reduced by 10%, the number of doctors who accept Medicare patients will decline by 6%." This is an objective conclusion that can be tested and verified by analysis. Making health care "free" is a political policy choice. What that policy choice would do in the marketplace is economics. The emergence of this debate about "fairness" would become known as the Progressive Era.

Some historians put the beginning of the Progressive Era as early as the 1880's, or to passage of the Sherman Anti-Trust Act of 1890. During this 30 year period before the outbreak of World War One in 1914 the social debate concerning child labor laws, women's suffrage, health, welfare, working conditions, and growing concern for the overall "fairness" of capitalism was gaining popular acceptance and political momentum, but the public debt burden on the economy, as a corollary for social spending, continued to decline from about 12% of GDP to less than 8% by 1915. The idea of "fairness" just did not make significant inroads into government policy.

It would take a near collapse of the economy in the 1930's before the original intent of the commerce clause in the

Constitution would be turned on its head. The commerce clause would become to be understood not as a guarantee of free trade among the states, but as a source of federal power to regulate the economy. This transition in thought would take hold in the Progressive Era of the early 20th Century, and reach its full expression with the New Deal in the 1930's, and in the enactment of the civil rights legislation of the 1960's.

For more than two hundred years the interpretation of the Constitution as a blueprint for prosperity has actually remained quite stable. There has been no constitutional convention called since 1787, and only a relatively few amendments have been added to it, and many of those were unfinished business from the compromises it took to get it adopted. Even the reinterpretation of the Commerce Clause as a source of congressional power has mostly been a reasonable response to create uniformity and consistency in regulation across the country. In recent years though, over-reaching by Congress stretched the boundaries of the Commerce Clause to such a measure of absurdity that even the Supreme Court finally had to say enough is enough. We are after all, a federation of states, and the sovereignty of the individual states actually does matter if the principle of self government is to retain any meaning.

✧✧✧

Speculation & Markets

Free market capitalism is a dynamic system of change. Economists like to talk a lot about market equilibriums, the idea that the forces of supply and demand work together like the blades of a scissors to cut at a point where there is a single market price that incentivizes a seller to deliver just the very last unit of market demand to a buyer who wants it. It is the Holy Grail of economic theory that markets will clear, people will make rational choices based on the price information they see in the marketplace, and natural economic forces will keep things in balance.

But we know from history that markets don't always clear, people frequently make completely irrational decisions, price signals are often misleading, and things can, and many times do, go completely out of kilter for completely mystifying reasons.

This cycle of boom, bubble and bust is often criticized as an undesirable and somewhat malevolent characteristic of capitalism that should be snuffed out whenever possible. This is akin to curing hyperventilation by suffocating the patient, a classic case of the cure that is worse than the disease. I am talking about, of course, those occasions when the normal operations of the free market, the everyday tug and pull between fear and greed, and supply and demand, is suddenly and inexplicably overtaken by a speculative frenzy. Alan Greenspan dryly described it as "irrational exuberance."

Speculative bubbles are like hurricanes. If you want to bask in the warm sunshine on a tropical beach, they are part of the weather. If you want a robust market driven economy that creates wealth and prosperity, sudden and dynamic change will also be part of the environment. It is necessary. It is part of the ecosystem of growth and prosperity. But like a hurricane, even if you can see one coming, you often can't get out of the way fast enough, and even if you do everything right and survive, you may still be left sitting in the middle of a devastated landscape once it is over. But we always go back to the beach, and we always go back in the water.

Many people hold a dim view of market speculators, and proudly bear a grudge against those who profit by making a guess, which is all that speculation is, a guess about a future change in market conditions. In actuality, speculation plays a valuable and necessary role in making markets work by providing information to the market in the form of signals about expectations for the future. And in truth, everyone is a speculator.

Price vs. Value

Before we get into a discussion of speculation, we need to have a short discussion about the difference between *price* and *value*. A common definition of an economist is someone who knows the price of everything and the value of nothing. This is usually meant to be derision against economists, but it is actually a fairly accurate statement, if you take the time to deconstruct it.

One of the first concepts that any student of money and banking learns is that money is nothing more than an idea. We make money tangible by giving it a physical form. Salt, rice, gold, silver, copper, pearls, shells, beads, cigarettes, carved stones, and paper, are all forms of tangible money. Almost anything than can represent a reservoir of portable, tradable purchasing power at one time or another has been used as money. Today we don't even bother to give it a physical form. Today money is just a series of 0s and 1s in a software program. We don't even give a thought of what might happen when all the computers go poof!

If money is just an idea, then what is *price*? Price is nothing more than *information*. It is nothing more than a form of morally neutral communication that tells buyers and sellers what is happening in the market. An economist actually does know the price of everything. Value, on the other hand, is totally subjective and wildly subject to changes in the environment.[15]

Inevitably, after every big natural disaster some local television station will do a live remote broadcast excoriating in breathless moral outrage the poor guy at the corner gas station caught in the act of changing the numbers on his signs, and raising the pump price of gasoline. Evil price gouger! Profiteer! Despicable exploiter of mishap and misery! Is it fair to blame the gas station owner for a natural disaster?

Let's look at it from the gas station owner's point of view. Let's say our local corner gas station has 6,500 gallons of fuel in underground storage that he would normally sell to a 150 customers a day for three days, at a little less than 15 gallons per customer, and on the third day, he gets a replenishment tanker from the local distributor, and life goes merrily on.

---

[15] Classical economists struggled to reconcile the "water vs. diamonds" problem in the search to discover the "true" value of a good. Water is the ultimate good, it is essential for life, but so common it had no value. Before the industrial age, diamonds were useful only as ornamentation, but they had high value. - Except that the value of each could change dramatically under the right circumstances. A diamond in the desert is worthless, and it is water that is priceless. The "value" of a good is totally fluid depending on subjective conditions in the environment.

After the hurricane blows through, all electric power is out, the local refinery is down for repairs, the roads are impassible, and the gas station owners knows that instead of three days, he might not get a replenishment tanker delivery for three weeks. And to make matters worse, hordes of people start showing up looking to buy gas for their generators, and top off the fuel in their Chevy Suburban, even though their tank is half full.

Now who is more morally culpable? The guy in the Suburban who rushed out to buy 30 gallons of gas he didn't need, just so he could get it before somebody else? Or the gas station owner who doubled the price to try and slow down the depletion of his only source of income, knowing he might be out of business for weeks after the tanks run dry?

The point is, prices have no moral quality about them. The price of something is a piece of information that serves to communicate market conditions to buyers and sellers. If you can learn to separate what the price of a commodity is telling you about the market from how you *feel* about it, you are well on the road to sound economic analysis. For all you real estate agents out there, repeat after me: "seller determines price, buyer determines value."

Speculation vs. Manipulation

This is probably a good place to make the distinction between speculation, which actually serves a useful economic purpose, and manipulation, which serves no greater purpose beyond the enrichment of the manipulator. Speculation is good. Speculation serves a market economy by incorporating everyone's best guess about the future into an objective piece of measurable information called *price*.

Speculation is legal for a reason. It is the most efficient way to communicate information about expectations for the future. A farmer in Kansas planting winter wheat in October needs to know what the price of his crop will be at harvest the following July. Look at any financial news and market information website, and you can find a price for wheat that hasn't even been planted yet.

How can anyone know what the market price of wheat will be nine months before it is even planted? The point is, nobody knows. But there are people out there who are willing to make bets on it. We call these people speculators, and they buy and sell their guesses about the prices of things that don't even exist yet on something called the futures market. And like it or not, we need them.

The farmer can look at the posted price for July wheat the previous October, and use that information to make better decisions. If the price of wheat in October for delivery in July is too low, the farmer may plant corn instead. A low price tells the farmer "We don't want wheat, we want corn, or soybeans, or something else. Plant that instead."

If you still feel the need for some self satisfying moral outrage, then that should be properly directed not against the speculator, who serves a vital purpose in creating orderly market information, but against the manipulator, who distorts and obscures the market through misinformation and misdirection. Speculation is organic. Manipulation is contrived. Speculation reveals. Manipulation deceives. It is manipulation that is morally reprehensible. It is also illegal. But nothing is more American than good clean, old fashioned, raw bare knuckled speculation.

We now know that prices are just information, and that speculative prices are just information about the future. So what does a speculative price *bubble* tell us? A speculative price bubble is an orgasmic state of arousal, excitement, and finally a climax of euphoria about the future. However irrational prices get at the climax of a bubble, there is always a sound rational basis at the beginning of it. It means something *big* is going on. It means *pay attention!*

Price bubbles appear as a result of organic conditions. Just as the gas station owner changes the price of gas to reflect a current shortage, or the farmer decides what to plant based on someone else's guess about next summer's price of wheat, a speculative price bubble communicates dynamic information about expectations for the future. A price bubble says "Pay Attention! The world is changing forever and amazing things are ahead!" And for the last 400 years the future has been looking pretty amazing.

So just what, exactly, is a speculative bubble? For the quantitatively inclined, here is the economist's definition of a speculative bubble:

"A speculative bubble exists when the price of something does not equal its market fundamental for some period of time for reasons other than random shocks. Thus if P is price, F is the market fundamental, B is the bubble and ∂ is a random process over time, then P= F+B+∂."

"Although this seems fairly simple there are numerous complications arising in practice with this equation. The most fundamental is determining what is the fundamental. This is usually argued to be a long run equilibrium consistent with the general equilibrium. This equation may represent then a temporary equilibrium with demand temporarily not at its long run position due to the speculative dynamics, But if there are multiple equilibria the situation will be very ambiguous. Also the fundamental should reflect an expected value of the long

run equilibrium which is frequently unobservable with any certainty. Also it is usually assumed that the expectation is rational, but that is very much what is at issue here. Furthermore, the error process may be complex."

"For assets with returns it is generally thought that the fundamental should be the unique present discounted value of the expected future returns. However, one cannot impute definitively from returns in one period what rationally expected returns in later periods will be, which is the key to the difficulty in reality of separating out the fundamental from the bubble, even in this relatively simple case. This is known as the misspecified fundamentals problem (Flood and Garber, 1980)."

Huh? If you followed that, great! You can buy the book for $199 Dollars on Amazon. (And you thought this book was expensive). For the rest of us, what he said was, "A speculative bubble is when people buy something only because they think the price will go up, and then one day, it doesn't go up, and then everybody tries to sell their stuff all at once."

In the last 400 years we have had some really spectacular bubbles, and they all happened for a reason, and they all heralded a new age of explosive productivity and an optimistic promise of wealth and prosperity for the future. All but the most recent one, but we'll get to that later.

◇◇◇ **PART TWO** ◇◇◇

Seven Bubbles & Seven Busts

Modernity, it turns out, is bubbly. This is the story of prosperity: how it came to us, how we lost it, got it back, and lost it again. Every time was the same, and different. Every so often, once in a hundred years, or so, something extraordinary would come along that captured the imagination. Every so often, following the inevitable bursting of the bubble, we would say: ""What were we thinking?"

Booms, bubbles, and busts made the modern world modern. We are currently living in the froth left over from the bursting of the most recent bubble, and it was a really big one. We have been down this road before, but the journey is never quite the same.

Seriously, *"What were we thinking?"*

✧✧✧

Bubble One: Global Positioning
Amsterdam, Holland 1637

In 1637 Holland was gripped with Tulip Mania, a massive speculative bubble in the price of the bulbs of a flower originally imported from the Ottoman Empire. Why tulips? I have no idea; maybe because they were new and novel and imported. Whatever the reason, an irrational speculative frenzy in tulip bulbs captured the imagination of the Dutch public. What could possibly evoke such a frenzy of "irrational exuberance" for a non native flower?

In the early 1600's Amsterdam was emerging as the center of a seaborne trading empire that had been gaining ground since the formation of the Dutch East India Company in 1602. It was the height of the first great wave of globalization that permanently shifted power away from the Middle East and away from the overland trade routes to Asia. The Ottoman Empire eventually collapsed into chaos, and we are still living with the consequences today.[16]

Tulip mania was the first speculative bubble of the modern age. Every successive world dominant power, Portugal, Spain, Holland, Great Britain, and then the United States of America would assert dominant hegemonic power over the ocean's trade routes. European based seaborne trade had been developing slowly over a couple centuries, so what

---

[16] The collapse of the Ottoman Empire was a slow moving train wreck that took place over three centuries. It would be overly simplistic to conclude that the advent of Dutch seaborne trade routes caused the collapse by itself. But, the analogy is valid. Societies and cultures that embrace dynamism and change tend to prosper; those that do not tend to fall into decline.

was it that sparked the public imagination for trading tulips? What else was going on at this time?

The Dutch East India Company was the first modern multi-national corporation and the first modern joint stock company as we would recognize it today. For practical purposes, the modern stock company as we know it, was invented in Holland. Shares of the East India Company paid an annual dividend of 18% for the next two hundred years, until the company fell into bankruptcy in 1798.[17]

The invention of the modern stock company spawned a financial revolution. The world was linked in a global trade network based on ship traffic over the oceans that touched every great civilization, as far away as Japan, and all of the New World. And now the Dutch had discovered the key financial innovation to fully exploit it: portable, tradable, ownership shares that allowed huge amounts of money and capital to be accumulated to operate a global enterprise.

The first world atlas with a fairly accurate geography of the globe appeared about 1570. The rudiments of the first global positioning system based on accurate time keeping and the geometry of the angle of the sun in the sky were still being worked out. But now capital formation could build the ships to move the goods to create wealth and prosperity based not on basic agricultural production in a local market, but on *trade*. Not subsistence level barter trade, not daily shopping at the market trade, but immensely profitable trade in rare and exotic spices from the far reaches of the earth. Speculators, entrepreneurs, and mercantilists were filling in the edges of the map that still said "Here there be dragons." You could make a

---

[17] Ames, Glenn J. (2008). *The Globe Encompassed: The Age of European Discovery, 1500-1700.*

fortune by trading, and everyone wanted a piece of the action. The first speculative bubble of the modern era was on. At the height of tulip mania in the winter of 1636-37 one tulip bulb could be traded for a thousand pounds of cheese.[18] Then one day, inexplicably, a buyer failed to show up and pay for his bulb purchase. Panic spread across Holland, and within days tulip bulbs were worth only a hundredth of their former prices. The tulip bubble had burst.[19]

Speculative bubbles during periods of revolutionary change in technology and economic productivity would become a familiar pattern for the next four hundred years. These booms happened for a reason.

Every great speculative bubble of the modern age was precipitated by a massive expansion in the productive capacity of the economy to create new wealth. All of the great historical mega trend booms that followed the invention of modern finance are associated with a sudden and dynamic change in some fundamental structure in the economy. An economist can easily describe these occurrences in elegant mathematical equations as shifts in the demand curve or shifts in the supply curve. But the math does little justice to the very powerful human psychology at work at the moment of perception that the world has been transformed. It is that *Eureka!* moment of insight when paradigms change and the kinetic instincts of innovation are unleashed.

The busts that followed these booms and bubbles were usually self-inflicted but also self-correcting. This history lesson will be important later, when we examine what happened after 1981, and the consequences that lie ahead for Generation Busted. It is important to know your history.

---

[18] http://www.damninteresting.com/the-dutch-tulip-bubble-of-1637
[19] Ibid

Bubble Two: Resource Extraction
New Orleans, Louisiana 1718

The City of New Orleans was founded by the French Mississippi Company on a few acres of dry land along the river in the delta basin that drains into the Gulf of Mexico. It was no place to build a city. The company's own engineers warned against building anything on the location chosen for the new capital of Louisiana, which claimed all land drained by the Mississippi River for the King of France. It was surrounded by swamps and prone to flooding and threatened by hurricanes. But it offered strategic control of one third of the entire American continent. So there it was built, swamps and floods and hurricanes and all.

New Orleans became the most sought after, most contested, and most strategic city on the continent. The city was ceded to Spain in 1763, reverted back to French control in 1801, and sold to the United States in 1803. The British Army tried to occupy it in 1815, but failed miserably in a lopsided slaughter of British troops.[20] The city joined the Confederacy in 1861, was occupied by federal troops in 1862, and remained in union hands until the end of the civil war three years later.[21] In 2005 the worst fears of the City's original engineers were realized when the city was effectively devastated by Hurricane Katrina, albeit almost 300 years later.

The year before New Orleans was founded in a Louisiana swamp, a Scottish businessman named John Law

---

[20] The battle of New Orleans was actually fought after the war was officially over. News of the peace accord had not yet arrived. The outcome of the battle did nothing to change the terms of the peace. However, it did prove the case that America was now a force to be reckoned with.
[21] http://en.wikipedia.org/wiki/History_of_New_Orleans

gained control of the Mississippi Company and secured a 25-year monopoly from the French government for all trade in the Caribbean and North America. [22]Law exaggerated the wealth of Louisiana with an effective marketing scheme which led to wild speculation in shares of the company's stock. A huge run up in the price was quickly followed by collapse and bankruptcy of the company in 1721. John Law wasn't necessarily a crook; he was just ahead of his time. Law was correct in his vision of New Orleans as the strategic key to opening the vast wealth of the continental interior. Unfortunately, the technology to fully exploit it, steam boats and railroad locomotives, would not be invented for another one hundred years.

Why would investors line up to buy vastly overpriced shares of a company whose principal asset was a small hump of dry ground in the middle of a swamp with nothing on it? Because of what it represented: resource extraction. The idea of a new French city in the heart of the English and Spanish possessions of the New World was irresistible. The logic was overwhelming. A French trading/commercial fortress city at the mouth of the Mississippi River meant that all resource extraction from the continental interior West of the English Colonies on the Atlantic Coast, and Spanish Florida would have to pass through French hands.

The city of New Orleans and all the lands drained by the Mississippi River claimed in the original charter of the French Mississippi Company would eventually give birth to the quintessential American character. Icons such as Mark Twain, Huckleberry Finn, Budweiser Beer, Louis Armstrong, Elvis Presley, and several uniquely American art forms: jazz, the blues, gospel, and rock and roll can all be traced back to a

---

[22] http://en.wikipedia.org/wiki/John_Law_(economist)

French flag planted in the Louisiana mud some 74 years before the country even came into existence.

New Orleans is the essential American City. Just the mere idea of such a city seated at the gateway to the riches of a vast continental interior foreshadowed the creation of a new national identity almost one hundred years before the battle of New Orleans. No other American city was so conceived. Andrew Jackson's victory in 1815 over the British sparked the imagination of an entire people, the idea that "We are Americans."[23]

The "Mississippi Bubble" was the first great speculative bubble of the New World economy. Speculative bubbles and financial panics would be a recurring consequence of the dynamism of a rapidly evolving economy as technology, productive capacity, and financial markets continued to evolve and move in and out of sync over the next three hundred years.

---

[23] It would take another fifty years to consolidate a true national identity as Americans. During the Civil War troops on both sides carried their state flags into battle and identified themselves primarily as "Iowans", "Virginians", and "New Yorkers".

Bubble Three: Steam Transportation
Baltimore, Maryland 1830

In 1792 the former English colonies created a free trade zone perched on the edge of the North American Continent. The acquisition of the City of New Orleans in 1803 and the British defeat there in 1815 secured the nation. The question was still open if the nation could secure the continent. A revolution in transportation technology would change everything.

In 1830 The B&O railroad laid thirteen miles of track leading west from the City of Baltimore upon which to test its brand new steam locomotive, the first of its kind in America. The railroad's objective was to connect Baltimore with the Ohio River and the West, just as the opening of the Erie Canal in 1820 connected New York City to the Great Lakes and made that city the greatest shipping port in America. Baltimore needed a transportation route into the interior of the continent to secure its own future as a great port city.[24]

When it quickly became evident that a horse drawn carriage over that vast distance was impractical, a radical new invention provided the answer: the portable steam engine. With Peter Cooper at the controls of his newly engineered steam locomotive, the first American railroad speed record was set when he reached the thrilling and unheard of speed of… 18 miles per hour.

This changed everything. In one summer afternoon on a stretch of track outside Baltimore, the speed of commerce had

---

[24] http://www.eyewitnesstohistory.com/tomthumb.htm

jumped in one instant by a factor of 6. On that bright summer morning the productivity of overland transportation jumped from the speed at which an ox could pull a wagon, about three miles an hour, to 18 miles an hour, a *six hundred* percent improvement in productivity.

Nine years earlier, in 1821 the United States had made another purchase of territory from a failing European Colonial Power, this time buying Florida from Spain. Only two years later, in 1823 President James Monroe delivered an outrageously presumptuous warning to the European colonial powers that any further attempts by European powers to colonize land in the Americas would be considered an act of aggression against the United States of America. Considering that only 30 years earlier these former English subjects had just barely survived a war for independence, it was an audacious assertion of new found American power.[25]

The United States boldly declared for itself hegemony over the entire New World, and now, with the steam powered railroad locomotive, it had the technology to enforce it. The race to close the American Frontier was on, and the United States of America would become not just a continental nation, but a global world power. The Monroe Doctrine is one of the longest standing tenets of American foreign policy, and was invoked by President Kennedy during the Cuban Missile Crisis 140 years later.[26]

The advent of the railroads was an exponential leap in the productive capacity of the economy. It also stimulated a series of bubbles and panics as investors and financiers rushed to capitalize on the implications of commerce on a continental scale at greatly enhanced speeds and volumes of cargo. It was

---

[25]http://www.state.gov/r/pa/ho/time/jd/16320.
[26] http://www.state.gov/r/pa/ho/time/jd/16321.htm

probably also the first time that a speculative bubble went global. In America, the financial panic of 1837 was brought on by speculation in Western lands. In 1846 at the peak of railroad mania in England the British Parliament created 272 new railroad enterprises in that year alone projecting 9,500 miles of new track. In 1857 another wave of speculation hit the US railroads.[27]

Fortunes were made and fortunes were lost, but the railroads were built and the economy was transformed. In 1861, at the onset of the Civil War, the Confederate Army was the first to use the railroad in modern warfare at a place called Manassas Junction. By rapidly repositioning troops on the battlefield they routed a Union Army of superior numbers at the battle of Bull Run. [28]

Only eight years later, in 1869, at Promontory Summit Utah, a telegraph signal wired to the track of the new continental railroad sent out a one word message to the world: "Done!" American hegemony of the New World was now unassailable. It was Manifest Destiny fulfilled.

[27] http://en.wikipedia.org/wiki/Railway_Mania
[28] http://www.nps.gov/history/hps/abpp//battles/va005.htm

Bubble Four: Electricity
Buffalo, New York 1901

Just as the revolution in steam transportation was closing the American Frontier and creating entire new industries completely unimaginable just a few years before,[29] a radical new technology was about to burst forth that would again revolutionize the productive potential of the economy on an exponential scale almost overnight. America was going to become fantastically rich.

In the 1890's a Serbian immigrant named Nikola Tesla perfected the 3-phase AC standard that we still use today for the safe and efficient transmission of electric power over long distances. In 1901 visitors to the Pan-American Exposition held in Buffalo New York were introduced to the astonishing site of an entire night skyline illuminated by electric lights powered by generators at the Niagara Falls hydro-electric generating plant over twenty five miles away. This was about to change everything.

---

[29] Almost as soon as the tracks were laid, chilled beef was heading East and fresh Oysters were heading West in insulated box cars cooled by blocks of ice.

Pan-American Exhibition, panorama view, from "*The Latest and Best Views of the Pan-American Exposition*", Buffalo, N.Y.: Robert Allen Reid, 1901.

The 1901 Pan-American Exposition was the crowning celebration of a century of laissez faire economic growth and a showcase for the new technological achievement of the age: the development of cheap portable, transmittable electric power. (It is also more commonly remembered for the other "shocking" event that occurred there, the assassination of President William McKinley. President McKinley attended the Exposition to deliver a speech on tariffs and foreign trade and was receiving well wishers in a reception line when he was shot twice by an anarchist, Leon Frank Czolgosz.[30] McKinley succumbed to his wounds within a few days, and Czolgosz was put to death a few weeks later in the electric chair!)[31]

✧ 1919 The Age of Prosperity ✧

When the United States entered World War I in 1917 the European Colonial Powers had already been at war for three years. Federal debt as a percentage of GDP shot up almost immediately, to as high a proportion as during the war for independence, and almost as high as during the civil war. The reserve capacity of the economy to sustain massive borrowing by the government in a time of crisis, and the ability to surge the army, would once again prove the awesome strength of the American model of democratic capitalism to the world. It was a uniquely American strategic weapon with which to overwhelm any enemy with a tsunami of war production. In 1916 federal debt was a miniscule 7.5% of GDP.

---

[30] Olcott, Charles. *The Life of William McKinley*, Houghton Mifflin company, Boston, 1916, p. 313-317

[31]

http://ublib.buffalo.edu/libraries/exhibits/panam/law/execution.html#note4

Two years later, it was 35% of GDP. It is amazing how quickly the US economy ramped up for war time expenditures.

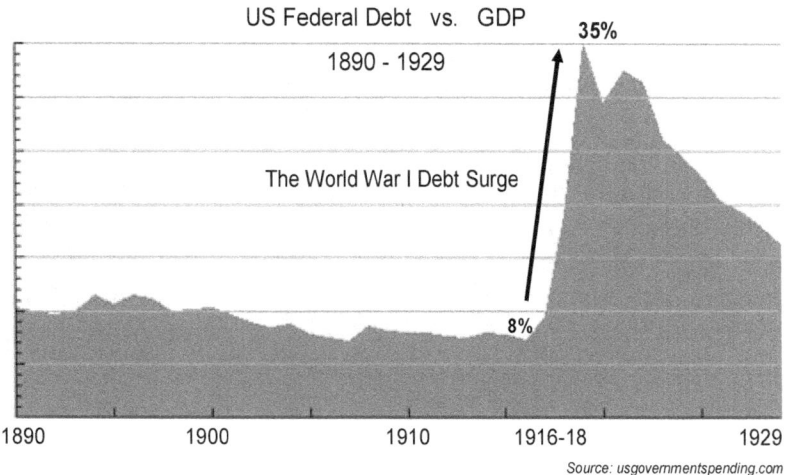

US Federal Debt vs. GDP

1890 - 1929

The World War I Debt Surge

35%

8%

1890   1900   1910   1916-18   1929

Source: usgovernmentspending.com

But what is truly astonishing, is the breakneck pace of change and expansion that transformed America between 1919 and 1929. The "Roaring Twenties" were called that for a reason. The decade between 1919 and 1929 saw the most dramatic sustained explosion in productivity gains this country has ever seen in our entire history. Almost every major aspect of modern life that we so casually take for granted today was either conceived or perfected in this one massive super nova of innovation and technological change.

In 1919 you had radios and cars. By 1929 you didn't just have radios and cars; you had cars with radios installed in them. In 1919 you had moving pictures and recorded music. By 1929 you didn't just have moving pictures and recorded music, you had full length blockbusters complete with high fidelity sound tracks, amazing special effects, and of course, the academy awards. In 1919 you had airplanes; by 1929 you had airplanes that could cross oceans and continents non-stop in a matter of hours.

In 1918 a world flu pandemic killed 20 million people. By 1929 a vaccine against whooping cough had been developed, vitamin D was discovered, insulin was known to regulate blood sugar, and penicillin was isolated. Walt Disney was creating animated cartoons, streptococcus was proved to be the cause of scarlet fever, and the Computer Tabulating Recording Company re-organized itself as International Business Machines, or IBM. The first television images had been transmitted in London, and Leica marketed the 35mm camera.

Robert Goddard was flying liquid fuel rockets, and NBC was broadcasting nationally distributed radio programs. By 1929 the all electronic television was invented, you could drive a car from Manhattan to New Jersey *underneath* the Hudson River, and physicists had proclaimed that atoms were made of particles, the speed of light was constant, the origin of the universe was a really big bang, and the Heisenberg uncertainty principle made things, well, uncertain. Margaret Meade published *Coming of Age in Samoa*, and German psychiatrist Hans Berger developed the electroencephalogram (EEG) for recording brain waves.

This explosion in innovation was reflected in the economic indicators of the time. The pace of innovation and economic growth in the decade following World War I was electrifying, literally. The rapidly expanding use of electricity in manufacturing was producing astonishing leaps in productive capacity. Incomes were rising fast and the frenetic pace of growth and expansion was justifiably reflected in a rising stock market.

It looked like the dawning of a golden age of prosperity and expanding wealth. So what happened?

✧ 1929 The Year We Invented Everything ✧

1929 should be remembered as the year we invented prosperity. America had become a rich country. Wealth was everywhere, living standards were rising, and great technological leaps were promising unimaginable prosperity. In the words of a popular song that would come out about four years later, America was *"In the Money."*

Unfortunately, that year is most remembered for a nasty little correction in stock prices that occurred late in October, only a couple months before the end of a decade that had produced an unprecedented era of economic growth and stunning expansion in American productivity and wealth. So what went wrong? Why did the stock market crash? How did things go so badly? What is the correct policy response to a stock market crash? In the classic laissez faire economic model, the government should do nothing. Free markets will self regulate and the natural course of the business cycle will sort things out. Under a progressive model, articulated later by John Maynard Keynes, the government should step in to spend money to purposefully stimulate economic growth. [32]

Later Milton Friedman and the monetarists would tell us that the worst of the depression was self-inflicted and exacerbated by a series of disastrous policy responses that choked off all the credit and liquidity in the money supply. This exacerbated what should have been only a healthy blow-off of irrational exuberance, and collapsed the economy into a

---

[32] Keynes John Maynard (1936) General Theory of Employment Interest and Money

total free fall. [33] Bad policy choices would defer American prosperity for another 25 years.

Today, any popular discussion about the direction of the economy, free markets, government regulation, tax policy, economic growth, debt and borrowing, whatever, you name it, at some point inevitably turns to the great stock market crash of 1929 and the economic collapse that followed. But it is one of the great popular misconceptions about the economic history of the United States that a bunch of greedy speculators drove up stock prices through wild and irresponsible speculation, leading to a spectacular crash that caused the great depression. Stock market speculators did not cause the great depression.

In 1929 the world became *modern.*   Ok, so not everything in the world was actually invented by 1929, but it is a pretty good analogy for the super nova in productivity and innovation that took place between 1919 and 1929. Stock prices were going up for good reason. The economy was growing, productivity was increasing and standards of living were rising.

---

[33] Friedman Milton, Schwartz Anna J. (1963) A Monetary History of the United States, 1867-1960

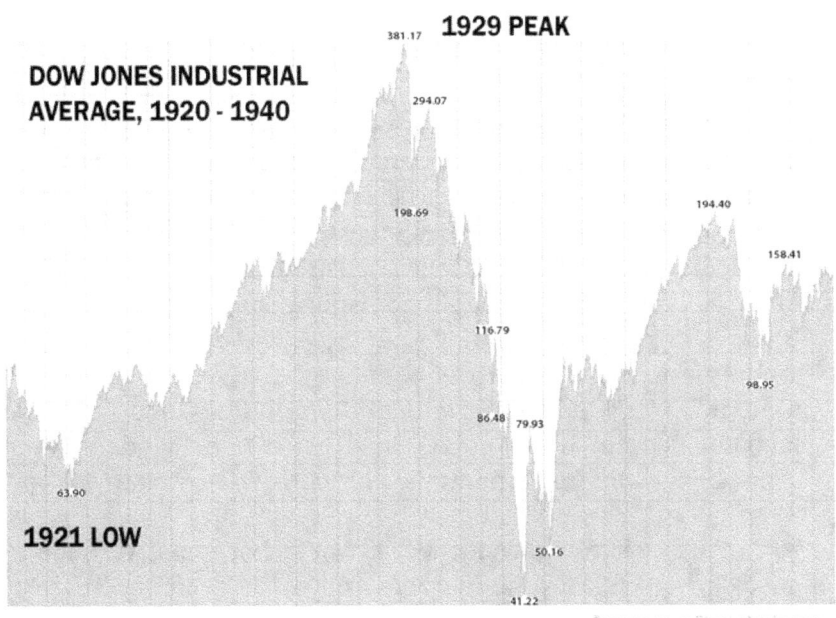

DOW JONES INDUSTRIAL
AVERAGE, 1920 - 1940

1929 PEAK
381.17

294.07

198.69

194.40

158.41

116.79

98.95

86.48   79.93

63.90

1921 LOW

50.16

41.22

Source: www.StockCharts.com

"The stocks that went up the most were in industries where the economic fundamentals indicated there was cause for large amounts of optimism. They included airplanes, agricultural implements, chemicals, department stores, steel, utilities, telephone and telegraph, electrical equipment, oil, paper, and radio. These were reasonable choices for expectations of growth."[34]

The popular notion that evil stock speculators caused the stock market bubble, the subsequent crash and the great depression of the 1930's is a myth. Stock prices rose 18% per year through the decade for the 1920's because the

---

[34] *The Causes of the 1929 Stock Market Crash: A Speculative Orgy or a New Era? (Contributions in Economics and Economic History) by Harold Bierman (Hardcover - April 30, 1998)*

fundamental growth in the productive capacity of the economy was creating fantastic gains in real wealth. Stock prices were rising because the proof of the prosperity to come was everywhere to be seen. Entire new industries were springing up; new technologies were rapidly expanding the potential to create wealth. A common share of Radio Corporation of America looked like a great investment. After all, everybody needed a radio, and a car, and roads to drive on, electric lights, and their own rotary telephone, right in their own home, with their own personal telephone number! The pace of change was simply astonishing. Borrowing money to invest in the future of America was a perfectly rational thing to do. Good times were ahead. People were going to live better. Modernity and prosperity were just around the corner. It was as plain as day.

So what happened? What was the speculative bubble in stock prices telling the market? Or was it even speculative at all? The decade of the 1920's was the most productive in our history, in terms of real percentage gains in output. No one buys stocks for the joy of holding the paper certificate in their hands that says they own 0.000001% of Michigan Power & Light. They buy it because they think the price of the stock will go up. And in 1929 it was a pretty good bet that stock prices were going to go up.

By the mid 1920's most of urban America was serviced by an electric power utility, and the potential of electric power to vastly improve the productivity of the nation's farms and factories seemed unlimited. Throughout the boom years of the 1920's the popular press reported almost breathlessly on the exploding demand for electric power. To appreciate the sense of the optimism and excitement this new growth industry offered to a nation hungry for growth and investment, just skim these headlines from the early years of the 1920's as reported in the New York Times:

SUPER-POWER PLANT FOR JERSEY'S NEEDS; Public Service Corporation to Add 200,000 Horsepower at Cost of $20,000,000. President McCarter Says Demand for Power Has Outstripped Company's Capacity, *Apr 14, 1923.*

ONE VAST POWER SYSTEM FOR WHOLE COUNTRY IS PROJECTED; EXPERT DISCUSSES PLAN Picture of United States of the Future Presented HUGE SAVING IN COAL With Electricity Available Every- where, Many Factories Could Move to Country, *June 17, 1923.*

POWER FROM COAL MINES BY WIRE SEEN AS THE NEXT BIG ECONOMY; Conversion of Fuel at the Source Would Mean Cheap Electricity in Every Home and Factory -- Pennsylvania Seeking Means to Work Out New Plan, *Sep. 30, 1923.*

DEMAND FOR POWER ANALYZED IN REPORT; Over 90% of Principal Urban Population Served by Central Station Systems, *Jan 17, 1925.*

YOUNG FORESEES THE ELECTRIFIED FARM; Chairman of General Electric Company Says Industry Must Turn Its Attention to the Problem and Provide Machinery to Promote Economy in the Production of Our Food Supply and to Simplify Rural Life, July 2, 1925.

PREDICTS EXPANSION IN ELECTRIC SERVICE; President of North American Company Sees $1,500,000,000 increase in Ten Years. NAMES FOUR MAIN SOURCES Homes, the Industries, Cities and Farms Are Expanding Markets, He Says, *May 2, 1926.*

Everywhere in the country real gains were being made in greater output with greater productivity. Living standards were rising. Broad based gains in a new middle class standard of living and prospects for a better life were actually happening. The way people lived and worked was changing, changing fast, and for the better. It is entirely normal and expected that stock prices boomed as a response to the dynamic earning power of these new industries. So why did it all turn out so badly?

A common misconception is that speculators caused the stock market crash by bidding up stock prices irrationally high, leading to the inevitable crash and the economic depression of the 1930's. This has been proven to be untrue. The fact is there was nothing in the economic conditions of the time to indicate that stock prices were "too high." *(See The 1929 Stock Market Crash Harold Bierman, Jr., Cornell University)*

We must remember that in sound economic analysis, *price* is just information, and a *speculative price* is just information about the future. And, by extension, a *speculative price bubble* is simply another form of information, just perhaps a little bit more dramatic in its consequences, but still not at all unusual. A bubble starts organically, accelerates, peaks and then dissipates in fairly typical pattern. Remember also, that whether a price is "too high" or "too speculative" is a subjective value judgment that gets in the way of listening to what the price information is telling us. A speculative price bubble is an organically occurring reaction to dynamic change in the economy. It is *normal.*

In the early 1920's the economy was still coal fired and stream driven. By the mid 1920's the transformation from a coal economy to an electric economy was adding millions of horsepower of productive capacity to the economy every year. New power plants were operating at near capacity as soon as they could be brought on line. Money was pouring into the stock market to support the explosive growth of this new industry. Investors were paying three times book value to buy utility stocks, and then they started buying more shares on margin to invest more money.[35] Buyers paid huge premiums for shares in investment trusts (today we would call them

---

[35] Buying on "margin" is using a small down payment to purchase shares of stock you don't have the cash to pay for. If the price goes up, you can make a lot of money. If the price goes down, you can lose more than your original investment. Gains and losses get exaggerated in both directions.

mutual funds) with borrowed money and bid up the price of utility stocks even higher, and it all made perfect sense.

So what was the price information telling us in the autumn months of 1929 before the collapse in stock prices? What was the speculative bubble in public utility stocks predicting? This:

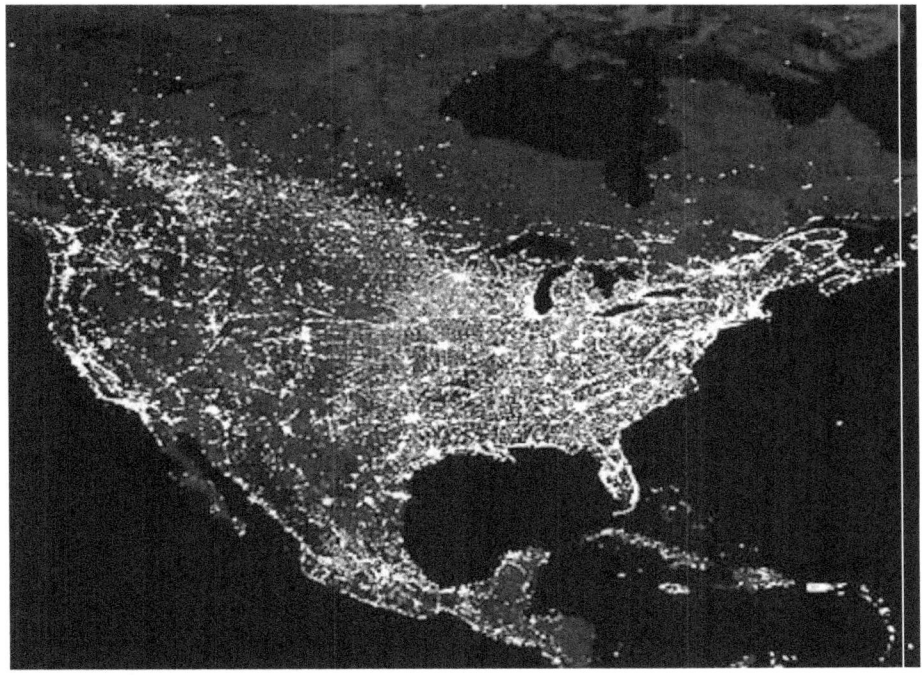

Source: NASA Image

In October of 1929 the stock price bubble in public utilities shares was correctly predicting a fantastic future of an unfathomable and incalculable increase in wealth built upon an all-electric economy. All through 1928 and 1929 public utilities were reporting record breaking expansion in the consumption and demand for electric power, with no end in sight:

OCTOBER SET RECORD FOR ELECTIC OUTPUT 7,900,899,000 Kilowatt-Hours Produced in the Month in Public Utility Plants, an increase of 14 percent. *NYT, Dec 9, 1928*

NIAGARA POWER CONCERN TAXED BY BIG DEMAND
Ontario's Hydro Electric Power Commission is now faced with the problem of a too rapid expansion of the market for electricity. Christian Science Monitor, *Jan 2, 1929*

ELECTRICITY RECORD HERE; Edison Heads Reports 11.6% Gain in 1928 in Metropolitan District. *NYT Jan. 14, 1929*

UTILITY WILL SPEND $34,500,000 IN 1929; MOST TO PLANT EXPANSION 1928 Electric Sales at 2,945,217,500 Kilowatt Hours, *NYT February 18, 1929*

POWER UTILITY TELLS PROFITS; Mr. Wishon said that during 1928 there was a heavy demand by agricultural customers for electricity for pumping due to the deficiency in gravity water for irrigation. *Los Angeles Times, Apr 16, 1929*

All through the 1920's the financial markets moved higher and higher, led by the public utility stocks and the dynamic transformation occurring in the real economy. The huge explosion in productive capacity and real efficiency gains in the transformation from coal to electric power was irresistible. One U.S. Senator even suggested making steam illegal!

WOODS DEMANDS ELECTIFIED RAIL SYSTEM BY 1931
Senator Sponsors Bill to Outlaw Steam, *Chicago Daily Tribune, May 2, 1929*

So why did the bubble break in the fall of 1929 anyway? The public mood was starting to shift from astonishment at the marvel of modern electric light as a novelty to the idea that distribution and pricing of electricity needed to be "*fair.*"

Investors in leveraged investment trusts and holding companies of public utility stocks panicked in the face of growing signs of government regulation and intervention into the electric generation and distribution market, along with a rising chorus of "expert" criticism that the stock market was in the midst of an "orgy of speculation". The bubble was going to break anyway, because that is what bubbles do, but what triggered it?

Speculative bubbles usually break when fear overtakes euphoria. And fear began creeping into the market in the spring and summer of 1929. Just two months after Senator Woods sponsored a bill to "outlaw" steam, in favor of an all-electric economy, another senator, George Norris of Nebraska declared his objection to private profit in the production of electric power. Note the date is just six months before the market crashed:

NORRIS URGES SALE OF POWER BY STATE; OBJECTS TO PRIVATE PROFIT Nebraskan Declares the People Should Have the Benefit of Electricity at Cost, Mar 15, 1929.

This is very scary stuff, if you are a Wall Street investment banker holding a lot of leveraged investments in public utility stocks. Especially since George Norris of Nebraska was a Republican. (At least until 1936, when he left the GOP to take Senate Chairmanships offered by the Democrats as a reward for his loyal support of FDR's New Deal programs, the Rural Electrification Act, the Tennessee Valley Authority, and FDR's New Deal programs). Later that fall a drumbeat of public comment by regulators and politicians derided the electrical generating industry for being *too profitable!*

Read Harold Bierman Jr., for a description of how the bubble broke when the mood in the stock market shifted from euphoria to fear. It is quite instructive on how subjective value judgments about prices being "too high" or companies being "too profitable" can play havoc with the psychology of a market that had every economic trend going for it:

Straws That Broke the Camel's Back?

Edison Electric of Boston

On August 2, 1929, the New York Times reported that the Directors of the Edison Electric Illuminating Company of Boston had called a meeting of stockholders to obtain authorization for a stock split. The stock went up to a high of $440. Its book value was $164 (the ratio of price to book value was 2.6, which was less than many other utilities).

On Saturday (October 12, p. 27) the Times reported that on Friday the Massachusetts Department of Public Utilities has rejected the stock split. The heading said "Bars Stock Split by Boston Edison. Criticizes Dividend Policy. Holds Rates Should Not Be Raised Until Company Can Reduce Charge for Electricity." Boston Edison lost 15 points for the day even though the decision was released after the Friday closing. The high for the year was $440 and the stock closed at $360 on Friday.

The Massachusetts Department of Public Utilities (New York Times, October 12, p. 27) did not want to imply to investors that this was the "forerunner of substantial increases in dividends." They stated that the expectation of increased dividends was not justified, offered "scathing criticisms of the company" (October 16, p. 42) and concluded "the public will take over such utilities as try to gobble up all profits available...."

....On Black Thursday, October 24, the market panic began. The market dropped from 305.87 to 272.32 (a 34 point drop, or 9%) and closed at 299.47. The declines were led by the motor stocks and public utilities.

The Panic

Once the panic started, it became almost unstoppable. Thus, the greatest expansion in wealth and opportunity in the history of the world came to a crashing stop. In less than nine years the basic industrial power source had shifted from coal to electricity, and literally transformed the economic potential of the country in one massive "Big Bang" expansion of productive capacity. And then we killed it, because it was "too profitable!"

Lesson: you should be very nervous when politicians start complaining about an industry that is "too profitable" or that "prices are too high" or that "prices are being driven higher by irresponsible speculators". (Remember that all through the summer of 2008 oil companies were being excoriated as being "too profitable" as oil peaked at $140 a barrel before crashing to $32 just a few weeks later. - We'll get to that in a later chapter).

But for now, as the objective analysts and good economists that we have learned to be, we know that prices have no moral quality of being "too high" or "too low" or "too" anything. Prices communicate information. That's it. If you only appreciate the price of something as subjectively "too high" or "too whatever", you will fail to hear the message the price information is trying to tell you. And in 1929 the prices of electric utility stocks were screaming for more investment, more capital, and more capacity to meet more and more demand. More! More! More! The speculative run up in utility shares, fueled by margin debt, wasn't screaming that stock prices were "too high" or that electric companies were "too profitable" or that Wall Street had gone insane in an "orgy of speculation" It was screaming loud and clear that the financial economy and real economy were out of sync. It was a signal to Wall Street not that the economy was overheated with speculative fever, but that Wall Street wasn't keeping up with the changes in the real economy. *Wall Street wasn't moving too fast, it was moving too slow!* Wall Street was misallocating capital into margin debt, rather than into equity, because it simply couldn't keep up with the demand for new investment in the new all-electric economy.

Real productive capacity in the economy is translated into the financial economy through capital formation and allocation. And in 1929 at the dawn of the Age of Prosperity, productive capacity was exploding in the real economy. It was the financial economy that couldn't keep up. Money was sloshing around; looking for a home in the electricity generation and distribution industry, and Wall Street couldn't get the money to work fast enough. So the leverage piled up instead of being invested in new equity issues of shares. Then the bubble accelerated, and then peaked, as bubbles always do.

It wasn't the debt or the speculation that killed the decade long stock market boom of the 1920's. It was the collision of grand standing policy statements by politicians, and the inability of Wall Street to keep up with an explosion of productivity in the real economy that killed the stock market in 1929. And in hindsight, most of the damage would have been avoided if the policy choices had been better understood. That is the real tragedy of the great depression.

✧ The 1930's: Global Militarization ✧

The unemployment rate in 1929 was 3.2%. For all practical purposes, conditions in the economy were about as good as good could get. Businesses were expanding, the economy was at full employment, and incomes were rising at the rate of 3.4% per year.[36]

Then it all went bad. And most of the pain was self-inflicted. The great tragedy of the depression was that so much of the despair of that time could have been avoided. There is a lot of scholarship out there that details the policy mistakes that exacerbated what should have been at most a correction into a full blown economic collapse. Knee-jerk trade protectionism caused world trade to go into rigor mortis. Credit tightening imploded the banking sector when the market was desperate for liquidity. Threats to nationalize private industries along with tax increases and mandatory wage increases threw investment into a deep freeze. These misunderstood policy responses turned the deleveraging of the investment trusts and public utility holding companies from a bump in the road into a colossal train wreck.

In 1930 the unemployment rose to 8.9%. In 1931 it rose again to 16.3%. In 1932 it reached 24.1%., and then peaked in 1933 at 25.2%, and stayed above 20% until 1936. The unemployment rate did not fall back to the rate of 1929 for *fourteen years*, until 1943, almost two full years after the United States entered World War II and put 8 million men and

---

[36] Source GNP: U.S. Dept of Commerce, National Income and Product Accounts

women under arms.[37] If it takes us fourteen years to sort out the mess this time, to clean up the wreckage from the collapse of the 2008 credit bubble, Generation Busted will be treading water for an awfully long time.

One of the great liberal conceits, and there are plenty of conservative conceits as well, is that the New Deal somehow rescued the American Worker from the deprivations of the Great Depression. In fact, most of the New Deal legislation did not come into effect until 1936, a full *seven years* after the economy collapsed in 1929. For the American Worker of the day, social security at age 65 was actually a pretty paltry consolation prize for a decade long deferment of the promise of a better life that was so close to being realized just a few short years earlier. The New Deal actually did fairly little to relieve the suffering of the working man.

In the interest of *"fairness"* it should also be noted that the Republican administration of the day did little to alleviate the suffering of unemployed workers, believing that the economy would correct itself without government intervention long after it was clear that things were going from bad to worse. But there had been plenty of boom and bust cycles in the economy before, and things had pretty much sorted themselves out on their own, so it was reasonable to assume the economy would self correct, like it always had.

By 1933, four years into the depression, it was beginning to look like there was no bottom in sight. The economy was still contracting and unemployment was still rising. Just a few years earlier, Capitalism was being excoriated because it was "too profitable". Now it looked like it might not even survive. The country was beginning to come apart at the seams. Laissez faire, the economic model that had built

---

[37] Ibid

America from a loose amalgamation of colonial outposts into a global power in the span of one life time was dead, and there was the real possibility that democracy would go down with it. But what would take its place?

1933 is also the year that President Roosevelt was given a copy of John Maynard Keynes' new book *The Means to Prosperity* which was one of the first to make a serious case in economic theory for counter cyclical spending by the government to "correct" the performance of the economy in a recession, with a description of something called "the multiplier effect". [38] If the economy would not grow on its own, then the government could spend money to make it grow. This new Keynesian economic model was more completely described in his most famous book published in 1936, *General Theory of employment, Interest and Money.*

Here was a theory that predicted greater prosperity not by government abstention, but by deliberate policy intervention into managing the growth of the economy along its ideal path. In the past, deficit spending had saved the nation in times of war. Could it save the nation from the Depression as well? Could the Keynesian "Multiplier Effect" bring back full employment? It actually turned out to work quite well, but certainly not in the way it was originally intended.

Most historians place the beginning of World War II as the first day of September, 1939, the day Hitler sent his modern combined arms divisions of panzers and Stukas across the Polish border and obliterated the Polish army and air forces in a matter of a few weeks. A more accurate date would be March 7, 1936 when Hitler moved German Army units into the Rhineland, which was supposed to have remained a

---

[38] Skidelsky, Robert (2003). *John Maynard Keynes: 1883-1946: Economist, Philosopher, Statesman.* p. 494–500, 504, 509 - 510.

demilitarized zone under the terms of the Versailles Peace Treaty at the end of the First World War. Hitler gambled correctly that his move would not be opposed by the Allies, and he successfully demonstrated to the German People his power to mobilize the German Army, and stir up patriotic fervor virtually cost free.

In a less Eurocentric point of view, you could make a strong case that the Second World War actually began even five years earlier, when on September 18, 1931 elements of the Imperial Japanese Army deliberately dynamited a section of Japanese owned railway near the Manchurian Border as a pretext to invade China the following day. This subterfuge, known as the Mukden Incident, was planned and executed without orders, but was ratified after the fact by the Japanese General Staff.[39]

Another candidate for the beginning of the Second World War would be October 3, 1935, when Benito Mussolini sent the Italian Army, with roughly 600 aircraft and 800 armored vehicles, into Ethiopia and in a matter of months slaughtered about 275,000 Ethiopian soldiers, many of whom were killed by the extensive use of poison gas and chemical weapons. The Italian Army lost approximately 500 men. May 2, 1936, Haile Selassie, the ruler of Ethiopia fled to England and warned the West. "Today it is us, you will be next." [40]

Or, you could pick July 17, 1936, when nationalist rebels in Spain staged a coup to overthrow a left of center government, resulting in a brutal Civil War. The conflict, largely viewed as a proxy war between the Communist Soviet Union and the Fascist Axis powers of Italy and Germany,

---

[39] James Weland, *Misguided Intelligence: Japanese Military Intelligence Officers in the Manchurian Incident, September 1931* The Journal of Military History, Vol. 58, No. 3. (July 1994), pp. 445-460.
[40] Barker, A. J (1936). *The Rape of Ethiopia*

raged on until the spring of 1939, complete with all the brutality, atrocities, and terror bombings soon to be visited upon the rest of the populations on the European Continent.[41]

Or, how about July 7, 1937 when the Japanese Imperial Army invaded China at the battle of Lugou Bridge, followed several months later by the Rape of Nanjing?[42]

But perhaps the real first battle of World War II was at Khalkin Gol in Mongolia, where the Soviet Union and Japan waged an undeclared war over the course of two summers in 1938 and 1939. In the summer of 1938 Japanese and Soviet forces engaged in open combat in a disputed border region of Mongolia. The following year General Zhukov, the new commander of the Soviet Siberian Army, annihilated a large contingent of the Japanese Army, inflicting as many as 45,000 casualties in a classic armored pincer envelopment tactic he would use again to great success against the Germans a few years later. [43]

The strategic significance of the battle is not well appreciated. Prior to this stunning defeat at the hands of the Soviet Armies, Japanese military planners had favored the Imperial Army in a "Northern Strategy" of expanding into Manchuria, Mongolia, and eventually Siberia in search of raw materials for its industries and markets for its manufactured goods. General Zhukov, Hero of the Soviet Union, ended Japanese ambitions in Siberia.

After this humiliating defeat the extent of the debacle was kept secret, and Japan's strategic focus shifted to favoring the Imperial Navy in a "Southern Strategy" focused on the

---

[41] Thomas, Hugh (1961). *The Spanish Civil War*. London: Penguin (3rd edition, 2003).
[42] http://www.world-war-2.info/battles/bt_17.php
[43] http://www.siberianlight.net/khalkhin-gol-battle-nomonhan/

conquest and domination of the Philippines and the countries of South East Asia, ultimately leading to the decision to bomb Pearl Harbor in 1941 and the inevitable collision with the United States.[44]

Based on US military readiness of the day, it was a perfectly logical strategy from the Japanese point of view. The Japanese Imperial Navy had the largest concentration of naval aviation in the world with a fleet of seven aircraft carriers and several hundred of the world's most well trained carrier pilots. The US Pacific fleet had just three aircraft carriers, and was just starting to get deliveries of the first of its F4F Wildcats, the Navy's first competitive carrier based fighter plane. [45] Considering the desperation of the early years of the 1930s, and how long the depression lingered on, it is quite remarkable how little the US spent on military procurement before 1939.

In 1930 the German economy was in a free fall, and gross domestic product collapsed to just about half of the output of the previous year, but rapid militarization of the German economy quickly replaced lost demand for goods, and by 1938 the German economy was essentially back at full employment, having put five million Germans back to work. So it would appear that a classical Keynesian economic stimulus of the economy through government spending did work. If not for the 60 million deaths that followed, and under different circumstances, we might simply have called the global militarization of the 1930's just an economic stimulus

---

[44] Ibid

[45] Marshall Cavendish 2005 History of World War II. Volume 1: Origins and Outbreak. Volume 2: Global War. Volume 3: Victory and Aftermath. Note: *For general information on World War II, this three volume set is an excellent source. Much of the information that appears in this book can be sourced here.*

program. Unfortunately, we did not spare ourselves the grotesque parade of horrors that the coming conflagration would inflict upon humanity.

Bubble Five: Manufacturing
Detroit, Michigan 1944

By 1939 the gross domestic product of the United States finally recovered to the level of 1929 a *full ten years* after the stock market crash. While other countries around the world had rapidly militarized their economies to bolster factory employment and keep up production, the US was still struggling to find a sound footing for the economy. While the worst of the economic collapse was over by 1933, the painfully slow economic recovery that was slowly taking hold through 1936 crashed again in 1937, and unemployment again exceeded 18% of the work force. [46]

America escaped the worst of the social cataclysms, revolutions, xenophobia and genocide of the 1930s, but not by very much, and settled into an uneasy period of isolationism while the rest of the world was arming itself to the teeth. By the time America became fully involved in actual combat after the Japanese attack on Pearl Harbor, the rest of the world had already been at war for *five years.* Today, after nearly seventy years of Superpower status, it is hard to appreciate the truly dismal state of the United States Army in late 1939 when a decade of conflict and conquests by expansionist powers finally exploded into an openly declared state of total war.

But on the eve of World War II America's enemies overlooked her most important strategic weapon: the reserve capacity of the economy to sustain massive government spending and a uniquely American ability to surge the Army. It

---

[46] U.S. Dept of Commerce, National Income and Product Accounts, Broadus Mitchell, *The Depression Decade: From New Era through New Deal, 1929–1941* (1947) pp446, 449

had taken the rest of the world the better part of a decade to achieve a full war time economy and maximize military production. America would do it in about eighteen months.

In 1939 the entire US Army consisted of six divisions of infantry, a force of about 175,000 men, and one Cavalry Division that still trained with horses. The army had practically no mechanized forces at all and did not have a single armored tank division that it could put into the field. For training maneuvers, troops used trucks with big cardboard signs attached to their sides that read in large letters "TANK."

By comparison, in 1939 the pre-war German Army consisted of a force of 1.5 million well trained men organized into 98 divisions, including 9 panzer divisions with over 2,700 tanks. This was a full two years before Germany was fully mobilized for war.[47]

In 1938 the US Army Air Corp received 160 new Curtiss P-36 fighter aircraft, which were obsolete the day they were built, and 291 more in 1939, for a combined force of 451 fighters that were already outclassed by more modern designs. In the same two year period before the "official" start of World War II, the German Luftwaffe took deliveries of roughly *7,500* modern fighters and fighter-bombers. In 1938-39 Russia produced *12,500* fighter aircraft, all thoroughly modern, but not as technically advanced as the German Junkers and Messerschmitts. Japan produced 4,400 fighter aircraft in the same two year period, and followed that up in 1940 with 4,000 more of an entirely new design, the infamous Mitsubishi A6M2 Zero.[48]

---

[47] Marshall Cavendish 2005 History of World War II. Volume 1: Origins and Outbreak. P 85
[48] http://www.acepilots.com/planes/specs.html

The US Army were so ill equipped for modern warfare that as late as January 16th, 1942 elements of the 26th Cavalry Regiment, an all Filipino unit, conducted a horse mounted cavalry charge against the Japanese Imperial Army while fighting in the Bataan Peninsula in the Philippines.[49] Later, after being cut off from re-supply, the army slaughtered its horses to feed the troops, a rather ignominious end to the glorious tradition of the iconic warrior-hero, the mounted horse soldier.

At the end of the 1930's the readiness of the United States to engage in modern strategic warfare on a global scale was truly pathetic. In 1937 The Army Air Corps had received a grand total of 13 B17 aircraft, Boeing's new state-of-the-art heavy bomber. A subsequent order for 50 more planes for the strategic hemisphere defense of Alaska, Hawaii and the Panama Canal was refused on the grounds that there was no need for a long range bomber with the capabilities of the B-17! [50]

In September of 1939, when it became clear that war was probably inevitable, U.S. National Guard units were activated for federal service under a declared state of national emergency. These units were so ill equipped and so ill trained they could not be used in sustained combat operations until late in 1942, almost three years later.[51]

In 1941 the United States entered World War II with an air force of fewer than 200 modern bombers and a few hundred modern fighter planes. What America did have though, was talented engineers, machinists and machine tools. The Boeing Company had developed the initial design for the B17 in 1935, and it took five years to get the design ready for military

---

[49] Gluekstein, Fred, Last Mounted Cavalry Charge: Luzon 1942, *The Army*, Jul 2005

[50] Cate, James L. (1945). USAF Historical Study 112, p17

[51] Lt. Col. George Eaton, US Army Command Historian, retired.

production, which as late as 1940 was running less than 40 bombers per year. (Although to be fair to the Boeing Company, this was due in large part to infighting between the various factions of the Army and Navy who didn't want the establishment of the new Army Air Corp to intrude into their areas of dominance.)

Contrast this tepid pace of development with the introduction of the P-47 Thunderbolt, which didn't even exist at the outbreak of the war, and went from design to production in less than eight months. Within a year production was ramped up to over 6,000 planes. In a less than a year US engineers and machinists had put into the air a fighter plane that was 100 miles per hour faster than anything else in the sky. It was fast, and had a massive 2000 horsepower supercharged radial engine. It was well armed with eight .50 caliber machine guns, offered excellent armored protection for the pilot, could carry bombs, provide bombers fighter cover at 40,000 feet, as well as deliver punishing ground attacks. It was rugged and hard to kill. It took a lot of damage to knock it down.

It was big and ugly, and nicknamed the jug for its stubby bottle shaped fuselage. It had none of the glamour and romance of the Spitfire or the P-51 Mustang. The P-47 flew in every major theater of operations in the war, and was absolutely devastating against its adversaries, whether in the air or on the ground. Over 15,000 were built, more than any other type of fighter in the war.

What is remarkable about the P-47 is that every other US combat plane produced in any quantity was already in flight testing at the beginning of the war. The P-47 was an entirely new design when it was ordered and outclassed everything else in the sky when it was introduced. It went from design to production in eight months.[52]

Aircraft production in the U.S. was a very small industry at the beginning of the war. In April of 1939 when the Army Air Corp finally placed an order for 524 new P-40s, it was the largest order it had ever placed for a US fighter plane. By the end of the war in 1945 American factories would produce well over *320,000* aircraft of all types, far surpassing the production of Germany, Japan, and Italy combined.[53]

U.S. factories gearing up for war production finally restored all the employment lost in the previous ten years, and for the first time brought in millions of women and African Americans into high paying factory jobs too. This would later create a groundswell for social change in the decade to come from which there was no turning back. Even though the US was the last major power to militarize its economy during the chaos of the 1930's, once it got going, American industry simply overwhelmed the rest of the world with a truly stunning output of military goods.

How did America produce so much war materiel from such a depressed industrial base so fast? The short answer is industrial talent: engineers, machinists, and machine tools. America successfully ramped up industrial production during the war years of 1941-45 in large part due to the fact that it had already done it at least once before.

In the 1920's automobile manufacturing was a uniquely American industry. In 1919, the year after the First World War ended US auto manufacturers were already producing well over a million cars a year. By the mid 1920s it was 3 million,

---

[52] www.acepilots.com
[53] Ibid

and in 1929 U.S. automobile production topped out at over 4 million cars in one year. US production collapsed by 75% to less than a million cars a year in 1932, the worst year of the depression. Industrial production collapsed, but the knowledge and capacity to make things didn't disappear. It just needed some one with purchasing power to start buying again.

But even during the worst of the global economic collapse of the 1930s the U.S. auto industry was completely and utterly the world's dominant manufacturing power. In 1930 U.S. factories produced over 2.4 million cars. By contrast, Japan produced just 19,684 cars that year, less than 1% of U.S. factory output, and all of these except 458 were produced in GM, Chrysler, and Ford owned factories in Yokohama.

Even as late as 1942, years after every other major industrial country had militarized their automobile factories for the production of trucks tanks, guns and munitions, more than 17 different US manufacturers turned out well over a million cars. No single company had more than a 22% share of the market.[54]

A potential adversary looking at the military output of U.S. factories in the 1930s could quite reasonably have come to the conclusion that America could easily be knocked out of an intense, but short conflict. America didn't have much of an Army, or Air Force to fight with, and what it did have was mostly obsolete. The U.S. Navy was still practicing 19th century battle tactics, and was busy wrecking the career of anyone who dared point out that long range strategic aircraft made battleship warfare a romantic anachronism.

---

[54] http://en.wikipedia.org/wiki/U.S._Automobile_Production_Figures

But in the private sector, America's designers, engineers, and machinists were producing state-of-the-art prototypes for technologically superior aircraft, ships, tanks, and weapons of all kinds through the 1930s. They just couldn't get Congress to buy them!

Even the best foreign made stuff had roots in American engineering prowess. The Russian T-34 tank, generally considered the best overall tank of the war, was based on an American chassis and suspension that the designer sold to the Soviet Union in frustration, after the U.S. Army rejected it.[55]

With perhaps the sole exception of the atomic bomb, every major weapon system and every strategic theory and tactical doctrine the US Army, Navy, and Air Corp used to win the war was developed in the mid 1920s and early 1930s, years before entering the conflict. When America finally entered the war as a combatant it already knew how to win. All it needed was the stuff with which to win it. Uncle Sam turned to its captains of industry with a very large purchase order:

2.4 million trucks, 324,000 airplanes, 88,000 tanks, 257,00 artillery pieces, 105,000 mortars, 2.6 million machine guns, over 5,000 ships, including 163 aircraft carriers, and all the raw materials to build them and transport them to the battlefield, including over two billion metric tons of coal, 397 million tons of iron ore, and three times the amount of oil produced by all of the other warring powers combined; and of course, eight million men and women in uniform to actually fight the war. Oh, and millions and millions and millions of cans of SPAM and millions of cartons of Lucky Strike cigarettes.[56]

---

[55] http://www.globalsecurity.org/military/world/russia/t-34.htm
[56] http://en.wikipedia.org/wiki/Military_production_during_World_War_II

How did we do it? Government spending on a massive scale; staggering stupefying amounts of spending and almost all of it with borrowed money. American factories finally had a customer with an unlimited appetite for huge quantities of cheap and reliable products of average quality, just the types of products American factories were the best in the world at making. This military spending spree finally brought the US economy back to full employment. Moral horrors aside, militarization of the economy worked wonders as an economic stimulus program in the 1930s for every country that tried it.

The real lesson is not that the U.S. produced more guns, tanks, ships, and planes than anyone else; it is how we did it. While every other major combatant power engaged in World War II struggled just to maintain economic output during the years of 1939-1945, let alone increase it, U.S. factories increased their productive capacity at an exponential rate, and essentially *doubled* the size of the U.S. economy in a little more than three years.

No other country revolutionized production, procurement, and transportation logistics the way America did during World War II. At the beginning of the war the U.S. Army finally ordered the Thompson submachine gun, which was already a twenty year old design. It was originally built as an assault weapon for trench warfare at the end of the First World War, but the war ended before it could be put into production, and no orders were placed. In the 1920's and early 1930's it acquired notoriety as the weapon of choice for bank robbers and mobsters, and by all accounts it was a fine weapon, especially when carried just for the purpose of intimidation.[57] Finally, on the eve of World War II, the Army started placing orders for it. In 1939 a Thompson submachine gun cost $350 to

---

[57] Ray Bearse, "The Thompson Submachine Gun: Weapon of War and Peace", in Murtz, *Gun Digest Treasury* (DBI Books, 1994), p.210

make, and as soon as the Army got its first shipment of the guns it was already looking for a replacement. The Thompson was complex, expensive, and required well trained machinists and sophisticated machining tools to manufacture.

In 1942 the M3 sub machine gun replaced the Thompson. The M3, nicknamed the "grease gun," cost $20. It was pug ugly, made of mostly cheap stamped metal parts, and was slapped together, not by a firearms company, but in a General Motors metal stamping plant that made headlight assemblies before the war. It was cheap and effective. Over 600,000 M3s were produced.[58]

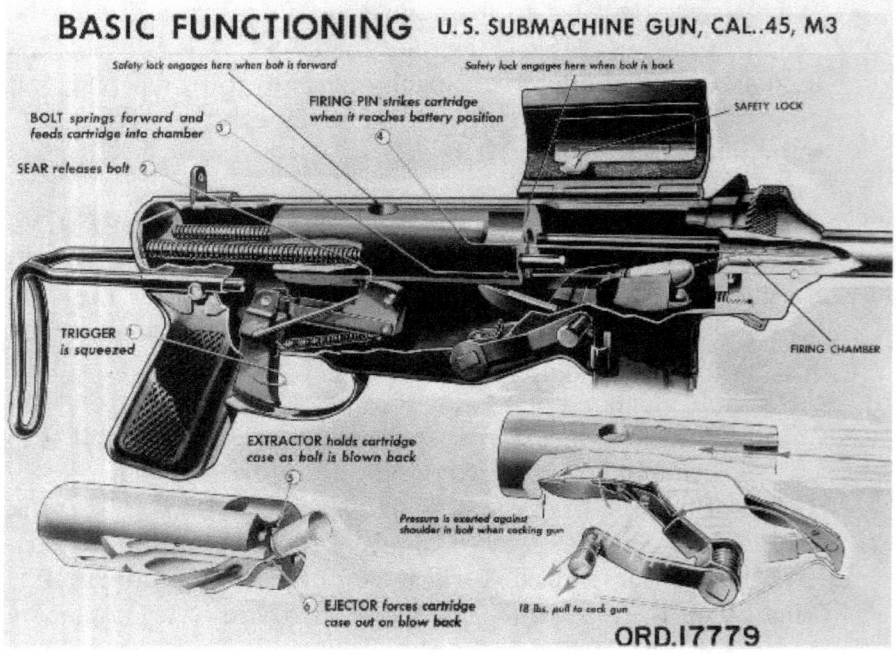

BASIC FUNCTIONING   U.S. SUBMACHINE GUN, CAL..45, M3

ORD.17779

---

[58] Ingram, Mike: *The MP40 Submachine Gun*

While other countries relied upon their professional munitions suppliers to design and build their weapons, which were often engineered to very high standards, the US government was turning away from professional armament manufacturers and looking to civilian industries to turn out overwhelming quantities of cheap, reliable weapons that were often less than perfect, but were good enough for the task.[59]

The best illustration of the revolution in productivity that occurred during the war is the miracle that took place in America's shipyards.   The ship building industry was scandalized when Henry J. Kaiser, a steel maker who knew nothing about shipyards and had never built a ship, was awarded a major contract to produce huge numbers of the new liberty cargo ship so desperately needed to get supplies to England and keep her in the war. [60] Ship building became ship assembly. Pre-fabricated modular sections shipped from steel mills and factories in 32 states reduced the build time for a standard Liberty class cargo ship from nine months to about 40 days. A few were assembled in less than two weeks. One was built in four days as a publicity stunt. They were cheap, ugly, and slow, but they could be built faster than the enemy could sink them. Henry Kaiser's shipyards built more ships and much faster than anyone else in the world, and at the height of wartime production the 10,000 ton ships were being launched at the rate of two and three a day, every day.[61]

---

[59] The M3 Submachine gun was issued to tank crews as a personal defense weapon of last resort. Front line assault troops still preferred the Thompson submachine gun or their shotguns for close quarter fighting. *Ibid* 48.
[60] Lavery, Brian. *Ship: The Epic Story of Maritime Adventure.* 2004, Smithsonian. pp317
[61] http://www.usmm.org/libertyships.html

school.mech.uwa.edu.au/.../libertyships.jpeg

To be fair, the ships were subject to occasional structural failure, and some instances are actually recorded where a liberty ship simply broke apart, or even sank due to brittle weld fractures. [62] But despite the shortcomings of an emergency war time ship building program it was nevertheless an exponential leap in manufacturing technology, turning the ultimate piece-built heavy industry into a highly efficient component assembly process. The pieces were just a whole lot larger than in the typical component assembly plant.

---

[62] http://school.mech.uwa.edu.au/~dwright/DANotes/fracture/maritime/maritime.html

But the U.S. didn't just invent the world's most efficient manufacturing economy in the 1940s; it also built a vast logistical capacity to move goods and people into the world's most extensive capacity for global distribution. This stunning revolution in the productive capacity of transportation should not be overlooked.

The threat of war greatly accelerated the pace of innovation and technological advances in weapons of all kinds. The explosion in manufacturing output by American workers is legendary and rightly celebrated. As is, of course, the truly heroic sacrifices made by airmen, sailors, and ordinary combat soldiers in desperate battles all over the world. But the sharp teeth of the dragon came with a very long tail.

The legendary offensive striking power of the U.S. Navy in World War II actually depended upon a relatively small number of ships. 22 fleet carriers, 8 battleships, 48 cruisers, 349 destroyers, and about 200 submarines. Almost all the rest of the five thousand ships built by American shipyards were required not to fight the battle, but just to provide transportation to the battlefield. There were the cargo ships, oil tankers, convey escorts, troop carriers, and supply ships for food, fuel, ammunition, etc., etc.[63] And while other countries struggled just to replace their losses of combat aircraft, U.S. factories were rolling out new planes literally by the thousands every month. Almost a third of these planes were not even intended for combat, nearly 100,000 of these was either a transport plane or was used just for training pilots and crews. Military trucks built by Ford, Chrysler and General Motors, gave the U.S. Army the ability to move overland millions of tons of supplies with unprecedented power and speed, all 2.4

---

[63] See http://www.history.navy.mil/bios/morison_s.htm, the official biography of Admiral Samuel E. Morison, author of more than 15 volumes on the history of the naval conflicts of World War II, for a comprehensive history.

million of them. General Eisenhower, Supreme Allied Commander, called the standard GMC 2 and 1/2 ton 6x6 truck one of the most important weapons of the entire war. [64]

The German Army relied on the professionalism of its officers. The Japanese Army relied on the courage and warrior spirit of the individual soldier. And the American Army relied on total, complete, and overwhelming material dominance of the battle space. We didn't just defeat enemy armies, we obliterated them. We pummeled their armies and their cities into rubble and then we made the rubble bounce just for good measure. America waged a total, global, and unrelenting economic war: a massive surge in the army, a massive surge in production, and a massive surge in borrowing to pay for it all. "Battlefield Expendable" became the vocabulary of the day. We would expend any amount of treasure to conserve the loss of blood on the field.

World War II was an unbelievable success for the United States. In economic terms, it was a pure super nova of wealth-building productive capacity. Having spent much of the pre-war years in isolation and under a false sense of security provided by two oceans, America emerged from the war not only virtually unscathed, but with the most efficient factories and most advanced global transportation capability in the history of the world. The rest of the world's economies were bankrupt, left with sixty million dead, with destitute populations living in burned out cities, and with nothing but the smoldering ruins of bombed out factories. At the end of the war in the spring and summer of 1945 there was a real possibility that the survivors of the devastation would either starve to death, freeze to death, or both, in the winter of 1946.

---

[64] http://www.globalsecurity.org/military/systems/ground/m35.htm

As a young expatriate executive living in Japan in the early 1980's I was suddenly taken aback one night while at the local pub. The crusty old Japanese accountant I worked for broke down, grabbed my hand with his, and told me his memories as a child of an American GI offering him the first chocolate he could ever remember. He told me "The Russians would have let us starve."

America spent its way to victory on borrowed money and emerged a global super power. It had taken just a little more than two years to get there. In April of 1942 America was shocked by the loss of the Philippines to the Japanese Army. 76,000 starving American and allied Philippine soldiers surrendered, having basically been abandoned on the Bataan Peninsula because America lacked the capacity to re-supply them. [65] Yet only two years later, in June of 1944, with still more than a year of fighting ahead, America was so confident of victory that Congress passed the Servicemen's Readjustment Act, commonly known as the GI Bill, already anticipating the millions of men who would soon be flooding back home and would need jobs in a post war economy. With the American economy now the most productive and efficient in the world, the promise of prosperity forecast by rising stock prices in 1929, and then deferred for more than a decade, was made a reality. In 1944 America invented the middle class. The economic transformation of the war and the GI Bill would sling shot the American standard of living to new heights of comfort and convenience for the next thirty years, until the first oil shock and recession of 1974-75.

But what about the hundreds of billions of dollars of borrowed money it took to buy all those tanks, ships, planes and guns? Why did America so easily absorb the financial cost

---

[65] Young, Donald J. (1992). *The Battle of Bataan: A History of the 90 Day Siege and Eventual Surrender of 75,000 Filipino and United States Troops to the Japanese in World War*. McFarland & Company.

of the war that had bankrupted everyone else? Well, first of all, we won. That always helps. But even England, a victorious ally, was left destitute by the enormous drain on the national treasury.

Productive capacity equals debt capacity. The more productive the economy is, the more capacity it has to sustain a debt burden over time. And by any measure of the transformative effect the war had on America's productive capacity, the money spent to win World War II was a bargain. America could now, hands down, out produce the world. The debt was simply vaporized by another gigantic explosion of economic productivity that fueled rapid growth, this time led by something entirely new; the American middle class consumer. Americans were ready and eager to buy again. And boy did they buy!

The Invention of Consumer Credit

In 1946, as fast as the country had geared up for global war, factories and businesses raced to retool and redirect production back into the civilian market. The economy was at full employment, consumers were flush with cash, and there was huge pent up purchasing power and demand for consumer goods of every conceivable kind. The most beautiful car ever made has to be the 1949 Cadillac Coup De Ville.

The iron curtain would soon descend over Eastern Europe, the United States would fight another war, this time in Korea to an inconclusive end, and the threat of atomic annihilation seemed like a real possibility. But in the looming cold war that would shape global political contests for the next forty years, America would soon unleash an unstoppable, ultimate weapon of economic warfare that no country on earth could hope to match: the consumer credit card.

Here was a brand new way for the new middle class to use their new found purchasing power that would propel the U.S. economy on a fifty year spending spree and take the idea of "keeping up with the Jones's" to a whole new level.

In 1950 Diners Club International introduced the first consumer credit card, and the age of the consumer was born. This revolutionary idea, that you could consume money you had not yet earned, started out as a status symbol for the privileged. By the time the credit boom ended in 2008, credit card companies were sending out new card applications to family pets and teenagers who had never even had a job.

✧ 1950's: The Disneyland Economy ✧

In 1974 a new sitcom called "Happy Days" debuted on American television, and for a ten year run on network syndication, became an iconic vision of an idealized American life in the 1950's.

America was ready for a liberal dose of nostalgia after the trauma of race riots, political assassinations, the shock of the Tet Offensive in Vietnam, another war in the Middle East, court ordered bussing, abortion, campus violence, bombings, domestic spying, sex, drugs, hippies, police brutality, airliner high-jackings, terrorists shooting up the Berlin Olympics, mindless degradation of American soldiers being spat on in airports, an oil embargo, price controls, a sharp economic recession, criminality in the White House, and the resignation of a disgraced American President. And that covers just the six years from 1968-1974. Oh, and by the way, Neil Armstrong walked on the moon on July 20th, 1969. It is no wonder that in 1974 an idealized version of suburban middle class life in a pre-Kennedy assassination, pre-Cuban Missile Crisis, Pre-Tonkin Gulf, pre-Terrorism world had such broad appeal.

In many ways, however, if you are old enough to feel nostalgia for 1950s you may actually have a good reason for feeling that way. The "Happy Days" economy of the fifties that would in 1955 create Disneyland, McDonald's Restaurants, the US Interstate Highway System, and then soon after Buddy Holly and Barbie Dolls, is unlikely to ever be repeated.[66]

Most likely though, you are one of the 4 million peak baby boomers that were born each year, and every year from 1954 through 1964, and have somewhat dimmed memories of the fifties. (Daddy had been away at the war, and when he came home papa and mama were gettin' busy). After the post war baby boom ended in 1964, it would be another 25 years until the number of live births in the US would again exceed four million in a single year, when the boomers themselves started having their own kids).[67]

If you were born after 1964, the fifties might as well be ancient history, because your world has very little in common with the first two decades post Word War II. If you were born after 1980, forget about it. You haven't even lived on the same planet.

There are plenty of excellent histories written about the fifties, and David Halberstam's book by that name is one of the best. It documents much of the social and cultural change, the origins of the civil rights movement, red scares, fears of atomic wars of annihilation or global extinction at the hands of intergalactic aliens, the emergence of something entirely new called the "teenager", all that subversive music, and all the rest of the turmoil hidden beneath the idyllic scenes of Mayberry RFD.

---

[66] http://www.ushistory.org/us/53b.asp
[67] National Vital Statistics Reports

Economically speaking though, the 1950s were about three things: oil, labor unions, and cars.

Oil

It is generally not well understood just how recent is the phenomenon of a world economy powered by oil. Coal was still America's primary energy source until about 1950. In the 1920's, 30's and 40's, even though the rest of the world was industrializing as fast as it could, oil too, was primarily an American industry. During the war years, no other country could even come close to the gushers of oil coming out of America's oil wells.[68]

At the beginning of World War II, when England needed to quickly replace lost merchant ships sunk by German U-Boats, the specifications for the new freighters it ordered from American shipyards included obsolete coal fired engines because England did not have the oil reserves to burn as boiler fuel in merchant ships.

It is also generally regarded that the U.S. embargo against oil exports to Japan in the spring of 1941 was a strong motivating factor leading to the Japanese attack on Pearl Harbor six months later. Japan was dependent upon US oil exports, and the embargo was justifiably considered a hostile act, although imposed as a response to Japanese aggression in Asia. With only a two year supply of oil on hand, the Japanese High Command was faced with the choice of watching its military slowly grind to a halt, or gamble big on a quick victory over the US Pacific Fleet and hope for a short decisive war. They gambled. They lost.

---

[68] http://www.eia.doe.gov/emeu/aer/eh/frame.html

Oil production was decidedly a major strategic advantage for the U.S. After being caught initially unprepared, within just a few months of Pearl Harbor, Army and Navy planes, ships, trucks, tanks and troops could go wherever they wanted to go, whenever they wanted to get there. U.S. forces could decide when to fight, where to fight, and how hard to put the hurt on. America alone produced three times as much oil during the war as all of the other major warring powers combined, 25 times more than Germany, and 160 times more than Japan.

In the 1950's oil went global. For the first time in history, consumption of oil in the U.S. exceeded the consumption of coal. Then, for the first time in history, America started to consume more oil that it could produce domestically. In 1951, just as the global economy was ready to enter the boom years of post war reconstruction, the Ghawar oil field in Saudi Arabia came on line. Discovered on the Arabian Peninsula in 1948, the Ghawar field is today still the largest known oil field in the world, some sixty years later.[69]

World demand for oil exploded. And for the next twenty-four years, from 1949 to 1972, in inflation adjusted terms, the real price of oil got cheaper...and cheaper...and cheaper.... In real terms the price of oil in 1972 was almost 30% less than in 1948.[70]

In 1950 world demand for oil was about 11 million barrels a day. By 1970 it passed 57 million barrels, a five-fold increase in demand, yet the price of oil in real terms was still falling. As businesses go, the oil industry wasn't even that profitable. The stuff was everywhere, and it was ridiculously cheap to make. OPEC was created in 1960, partly to try and

---

[69] Parra, F., "Oil Politics: A Modern History of Petroleum," (I.B. Taurus 2004).
[70] http://www.wtrg.com/prices.htm

stop the flood of oil production coming out of the Middle East that was threatening to collapse prices even more. The profit margins in oil just weren't that great. Even at the peak of the price bubble in 2008 when gas prices hit $4 a gallon oil company margins were generally no better than an average U.S. industrial company.

In the 1950's the real money to be made was in the U.S. auto industry. Cars were big and getting bigger, more stylish, more powerful and more fun than ever to drive. Cars, baby. It was all about the cars! ...and packaged food, and hamburgers, and theme parks, and science fiction movies, and for the first time, teenagers with lots of money to spend on all of it. We'll get to the cars, but cars need gasoline, and gasoline was dirt cheap.

The ramp up in world oil production in the last sixty years is nothing short of spectacular, and there is an almost perfect correlation to consumption of oil and a rising standard of living. No country on the planet has significantly raised its standard of living without quickly and vastly expanding its use of oil. We owe our very comfortable standard of living almost entirely upon the oceans of goo left behind by several hundred million years of dead algae.

You have probably heard this statistic before: that the United States, with 5% of the world's population consumes 25% of the world's oil production. I hope you enjoyed the party, because the party is over. The statistical evidence is hotly debated, but it has been suggested that sometime in the next few years world oil production will reach its all time peak, and then start to fall. The real battle being how fast new technology can be developed to slow down the rate of decline. Two things are certain though. One, the really cheap stuff is mostly gone. Two, the new stuff is going to cost more. Say goodbye to cheap gas, probably forever.[71] They didn't call it "Happy Days" without good reason.

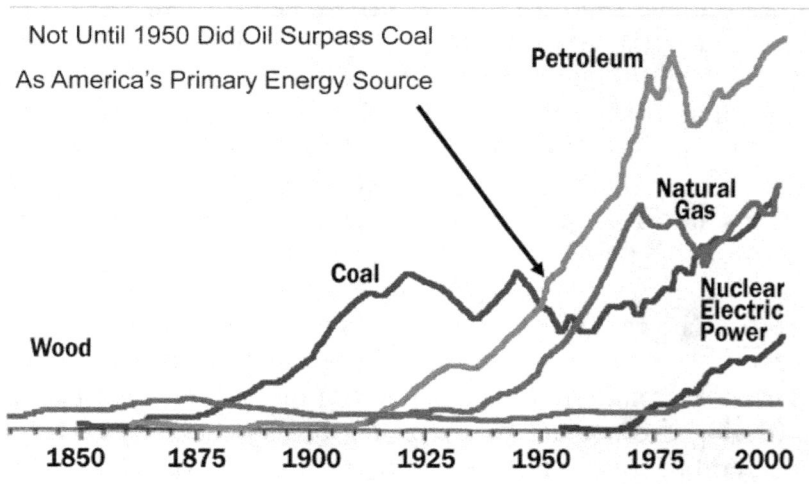

AMERICAN MIDDLE CLASS PROSPERITY
Floating on a Sea of Oil

Not Until 1950 Did Oil Surpass Coal
As America's Primary Energy Source

Source: USDOE

Cars

In the 1950's building cars in the U.S. was an insanely profitable business. During the war years of the early 1940's U.S. auto companies had built up a huge infrastructure of new factories and highly efficient manufacturing techniques, all paid for by government procurement contracts to supply the

---

[71] Prof. Kjell Aleklett, Testimony on Peak Oil before the House Subcommittee on Energy and Air Quality, Dec. 7 2005

war effort. When the war ended car companies raced to retool for civilian production, and within a year or two were again pushing out millions of cars. Automobile production in 1949 finally smashed the production record set in 1929 by a million units.[72]

After twelve years of depression and five years of war, America went car crazy. Never mind that the cars were technologically primitive, even for the day. Most of the cars produced during the 1950's were built with engines, suspensions, and transmissions originally designed in the 1930's. (In 1937 Chevrolet introduced the second generation of its in-line six cylinder engine, which had originally debuted in 1929. The Chevy straight-six stayed in production until 1963). America wanted cars: big, flashy chrome dipped monster land boats. And no one could make them like Detroit.[73]

In the post war economy auto companies were earning almost double the profit margins of the average industrial company in America. Weaker companies that couldn't keep up were quickly put out of business or consolidated into the "Big Three"; Ford, GM, and Chrysler established almost total monopoly pricing power over the rest of the industry.[74]

By the time President Eisenhower signed the Federal Highway Act that created the National Defense Interstate Highway System in 1956, (Yes, it's true. In the 1950's Interstate Highways were considered a matter of national security), Americans were buying eight million cars a year, essentially all of them Ford, Chrysler or GM products.[75]

---

[72] Automotive News Market Data Book, various years,

[73] Ibid
[74] http://www.econ.ucdavis.edu/faculty/fzfeens/trans/Transport
[75] Ibid

Cheap oil, cheap cars, and new highway construction all across the country was keeping Americans employed by the millions. New highways meant new suburban towns and a booming construction market for new homes. New homes meant new appliances, new refrigerators, new televisions, new furniture, and new babies.

In 1952 when General Motors President famously said "What is good for General Motors is good for America" it was hardly spoken in arrogance. He was simply making a factual observation that the new American middle class prosperity being celebrated all across the country was largely a direct result of the huge profits being generated in the car business, and the millions of jobs it created.

And what about all that debt that had piled up to finance government spending during the 1930's and the mountains of debt left over from the cost of World War II? It simply disappeared under a rising tide of unprecedented economic growth sustained by falling oil prices and manufacturing profits. From a peak of 120% of GDP in 1946, U.S. government debt as a percentage of the gross domestic product declined steadily for the next 30 years, reaching its lowest point in 1980, when increases in defense spending and tax cuts during the Presidency of Ronald Reagan reversed the downward trend.

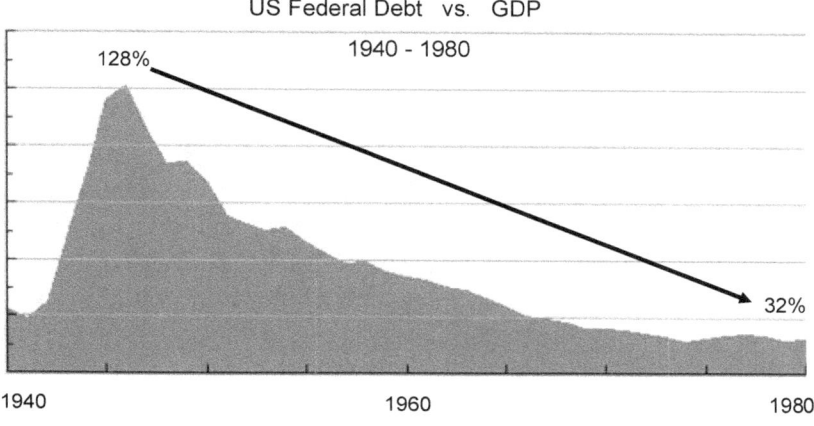

The 33 year period between 1946 and 1979 was, economically speaking, the perfect Disneyland fairy tale. No wonder the baby boomers grew up with unrealistic expectations of instant gratification and an exaggerated sense of entitlement. The next 33 years are not likely to be so kind to them.

Labor Unions

The history of the labor movement in the U.S. prior to World War II is marked by a long series of protracted and bloody battles. It is a story of cracked heads and violent confrontations in front of the factory gates. Before 1935 less than 15% of the private sector workforce was represented by trade union membership. It wasn't until the National Labor Relations Act became law that year, which outlawed the most egregious practices that had been used to suppress the labor movement, that trade union representation and collective bargaining began to substantially take root in American factories.[76]

In the post war years of huge profit margins and monopoly market share, (everybody else's factories had been bombed out of existence) orderly and peaceful labor relations suited the purposes of both the major auto companies as well as the big union bosses. The companies soon developed a predictable pattern of contract negotiations called, surprisingly enough, the "pattern bargain agreement."[77] The unions would target one company for increases in wages and benefits based on a predictable formula that allowed for increases in pay based on a factor of productivity improvement in the factory and a component that reflected any change in the overall cost of living. This created a comfortable arrangement whereby the unions could deliver consistent increases in pay and benefits to its members, and the auto companies were able to minimize any variability in labor costs among the "Big Three" such that no company could achieve a labor cost advantage over any of its competitors.[78]

All through the 1950's and well into the 1960's, despite rising labor costs and increases in pay and benefits, the U.S. auto industry continued to deliver stellar profits far in excess of the average industrial company.[79] Trade union representation of the labor force increased steadily until reaching its peak in

---

[76]US Department of Labor Bureau of Labor Statistics Leo Troy & Neil Sheflin, *Union Sourcebook*

LABOR RELATIONS IN THE UNIONIZED AUTOMOBILE ASSEMBLY INDUSTRY IN THE UNITED STATES: 1961-2006. Richard N. Block, Professor School of Labor and Industrial Relations Michigan State University

[77] http://www.econ.ucdavis.edu/faculty/fzfeens/trans/Transport-lecture6.pdf

[78] Block, Richard

[79] Automotive News Market Data Book, various years,

1960, when almost half of U.S. workers belonged to a trade union. After 1960 American labor would never have it so good. From that peak in 1960, union representation in the workplace steadily declined every year for the next fifty years. Today, private trade unions represent about 9% of the U.S. workforce, about the same as they did in 1909, one hundred years ago. The glory days of the industrial labor union disappeared as quickly as they had come.[80]

You may have romantic visions of the heroic union organizer sacrificing life and limb for the cause of the working man, but the fact is it was the unique combination of total U.S. manufacturing dominance over the world's economy, the car companies' almost monopoly power to set wage rates and pass along higher labor costs with price increases, along with a world glut of cheap oil that made the labor movement's successes in the 1950's possible. Management wanted docile labor relations and negotiated increases in wages and benefits because their monopoly pricing power and the stunning gains in factory productivity achieved in the previous ten years afforded it. The unions were simply along for the ride. When profitability in American manufacturing disappeared, so did the unions.[81]

The ignominious bankruptcy of General Motors in 2009 was the last gasp of a dinosaur that failed to evolve past an age of monopoly market share and an era of cheap oil we will never see again, and the private sector labor union died with it. Today the only union membership that is alive and well is the union membership of government employees. The new American Aristocrat is a public employee with a government pension. These privileged are most likely the only ones who

---

[80] US Department of Labor Bureau of Labor Statistics Leo Troy & Neil Sheflin, *Union Sourcebook*
[81] Ibid

will escape the burden that is going to be laid upon the backs of Generation Busted.

✧ 1960's: Alerted Consciousness ✧

America entered the 1960's with a confident young President dripping with rock-star sex appeal. Camelot, as John Kennedy and his round table of young advisors was called with an uncontrived romanticism, seems quaint and naïve today, but the optimism and idealism was genuinely felt. America could go anywhere, and could pay any price, and America was going to change the world and fill it with goodness and light.

The scope and expanse of American ambition heading into the 1960's was beyond audacious. It was grandiose on a cosmic scale. America wasn't just going to fill the world with the righteous light of democratic capitalism, America would stamp out racism. America would end poverty. America would stop the spread of godless communism. America would build a "Great Society." America would build rockets and fly them to the moon!

About the only part of that plan that went on schedule was the going to the moon part. On Christmas Eve, 1968 while in lunar orbit on board Apollo 8, astronaut William Anders snapped NASA image AS8-14-2383. More poetically known as "Earthrise," it became the iconic photograph of the age, and came to symbolize the seismic shifts that were taking place in the consciousness of the American public.

This one photograph, taken by a NASA math geek, did more to alter the consciousness of the American Public than all the hippie peace and love crap put together. Stupid hippies. The following year the Apollo 9 mission fulfilled President Kennedy's promise to land a man on the moon and return him safely to the earth before the decade was out. In the next three years America's astronauts would make eight more trips to the moon, the last one in December of 1972. No one has been back since.

In the midst of the cultural earthquake that was the 1960's, the cold war, the civil rights movement, the escalation of the war in Vietnam, race riots in American cities, the idiotic hallucinogenic-haze induced "summer of love," the chaos of the anti-war movement, and the turmoil and tragedy of the Presidential campaign of 1968, another earthquake was shaking the very foundation of the US economy down to the bedrock of American middle class prosperity. Amidst all the chaos, it went almost completely unnoticed.

In 1968 the earthquake that was off the seismograph was the convergence of two trend lines that signaled the end of seventy years of American manufacturing dominance over the rest of the world, and the end of predictable, reliable increases in wages and benefits for American labor.

In 1968, for the first time since the end of World War II, profit margins at the "Big Three" U.S. automakers fell below the U.S. average of about a 10% profit margin for an industrial company, and the market share of imported foreign made cars rose above 10% for the first time. In 1968, for the first time ever, one in ten cars sold in the United States was not made in an American factory by American workers. [82]

Seventy years of American manufacturing dominance of the auto industry ended forever, and at first it was hardly noticed. It had taken twenty years of post war reconstruction before foreign auto makers could penetrate 10% of the U.S.

---

[82] http://www.econ.ucdavis.edu/faculty/fzfeens/trans/Transport-lecture6.pdf

auto market. It only took 7 more years, until 1975, to reach almost 20%, and only 5 more years to reach almost 30%. By 1980 almost 1 in every 3 cars sold in America was a foreign made car.[83]

In less than twelve years the power and sway of the U.S. auto industry collapsed from one of the most reliably profitable business models in American history to the brink of disaster.

Japanese cars were cheaper and better made than American cars. In the late 1960's the marketing strategies of the U.S. companies seemed limited to cramming the biggest possible engine onto the lightest possible chassis and selling cars based on their neck-snapping performance. The muscle cars of the late 1960's and early 1970's are fondly remembered for their excitement and sex appeal, but they also sucked down gas, were technologically obsolete, and tended to fall apart rather quickly.

After the oil shock and recession of 1974-75 U.S. auto makers struggled to retool to make smaller more fuel efficient cars, but the Japanese cost advantages in smaller cars was insurmountable and devastated the sales and profits of the U.S. auto makers.[84]

Chrysler slid into bankruptcy and needed a guaranteed government loan to stay afloat, which it received probably because it was also a leading defense contractor. Ford and the United Auto Workers Union petitioned the U.S. government for relief, and from 1981 through 1985 U.S. auto makers hid

---

[83] Ibid

[84] Ibid

behind a protectionist shield of "voluntary" export quotas that finally restored the profitability of the U.S. companies.[85]

U.S. world dominance in auto manufacturing was lost forever, and for the next forty years the "Big Three" scrambled desperately to improve the quality of their cars and find a profitable niche for their products. Union contracts were no longer about reliable increases in pay and benefits, but shifted to negotiating job security in an industry that was permanently shedding high paying union jobs. The business model that built the American middle class was in serious trouble. 1981 also was the first year Generation Busted babies started being born.

✧ 1970's: The Other Shoe Drops ✧

On April 22, 1970 approximately 20 million Americans celebrated "Earth Day" to demonstrate against environmental degradation and raise awareness to promote the goal of healthy and "sustainable" economic growth. The environmental movement quite correctly criticized the degradation of air quality and water resources that accompanied twenty years of post war break neck economic growth. Poisoned air and poisoned water was quite literally killing people, and it needed to be cleaned up. That much was true. About almost everything else, they were dead wrong.[86]

Eighty percent of the world's animal species did not go extinct, four billion people, including 1/3 of the population of the United States, did not die of starvation, air pollution did not reduce the amount of sunlight reaching the Earth's surface by half, causing major global cooling, (yes, I said global cooling) and the Earth's temperature did not drop by 11 degrees by the

---

[85] Ibid
[86] *Bailey, Richard.* (May 2000) Earth Day Then And Now, print edition
http://reason.com/archives/2000/05/01/earth-day-then-and-now

year 2000 leading to the onset of a new global ice age. Yes that's right, in 1970 serious people were worried about global *cooling*.

And the alarm was raised that if the trend of increasing global oil consumption was not immediately reversed, the world's total supply of crude oil would be exhausted forever by the year 2000. I did not make this stuff up. Seriously though, environmental degradation really had become a legitimate public health issue worthy of a robust debate and a public policy response. But the alarmism was over the top. Americans had achieved a very high material standard of living, and now they wanted a higher quality of life too. There is certainly nothing wrong with that, but the alarmism that was passed off as science was largely misplaced.

The dire predictions of "peak oil" might actually come true. They just missed it by about 100 years or so. In 1950 the world was consuming about 11 million barrels a day. In 1970 it was up to 57 million barrels a day. Today, world oil consumption is up to 85 million barrels a day, and likely to go higher still. Global demand has grown 9-fold in fifty years, and production has kept pace with demand all the way. In the last 140 years of industrial scale oil production the world average price of oil in constant dollars has remained essentially flat at around $22 a barrel. Any of the huge spikes in oil prices or disruptions in supply is almost perfectly correlated to political events, not shortages in production. In times of war, oil prices go up. In times of relative peace, oil prices go down, but there has never, ever been a true "shortage" of oil in the real economic sense of the word.[87]

Eventually the productivity of all oil fields does decline. But we continue to invent new recovery technologies

---

[87] http://www.wtrg.com

that extend the life of oil fields and their productive capacity. It may mean higher prices as oil production gets marginally more expensive, and absent new discoveries on the scale of 3 or 4 Saudi Arabia sized fields, it is likely that world oil production will eventually reach an all time peak, and then start to slowly decline. The jury is still out if innovation can make up the difference in the inevitable decline in the productivity of known resources.

The productivity of U.S. oil wells peaked in 1972 and has declined ever since.[88]

US OIL WELL PRODUCTIVITY

As the productivity of US oil wells began to decline, so did total production.[89]

---

[88] US Department of Energy

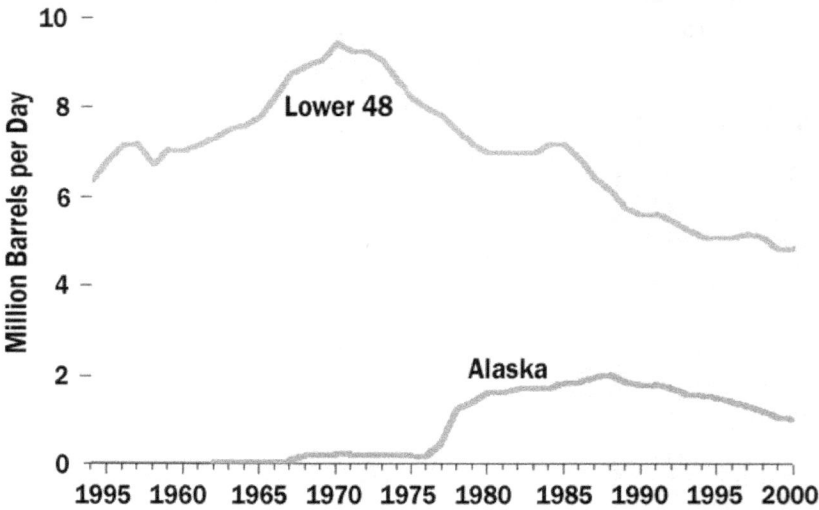

U.S. Lower 48 and Alaskan Crude Oil Production

And relatively cheap imported oil made up the difference.

It should be noted that the decline in U.S. domestic oil production has very little to do with the actual quantity of resources that are available. There are vast deposits of oil in the Green River Basin in Colorado, in the Bakken Formation in North Dakota and Wyoming, and of course in Alaska and the off shore continental shelf of California and the Gulf of Mexico. The resources are there, and so is the technology to exploit them. Declining oil production in the US has more to do with environmental politics than a lack of capability.

But the real reason is lifting cost. In pure economic terms, importing low cost Middle East oil was just cheaper.

---

[89] Ibid

U.S. Energy Supplies: Vulnerable and Getting Worse

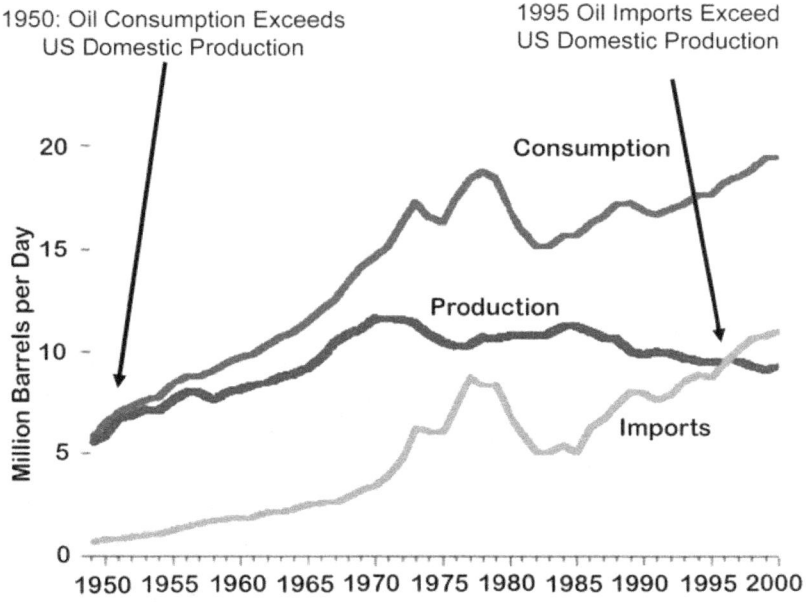

1950: Oil Consumption Exceeds
US Domestic Production

1995 Oil Imports Exceed
US Domestic Production

The Trend Lines Go Bad

In 1996, just as Generation Busted babies started becoming teenagers, America imported more oil than it produced domestically for the first time. When trends lines cross, watch out! It usually means big changes are coming.

Middle class living standards in the U.S. after World War II were built on the pillars of an era of unprecedented American dominance in manufacturing, lots of cheap and plentiful oil, and relatively peaceful trade union representation of the American workforce. All three of these pillars of prosperity would come under intense pressure during the late 1970's.

In 1968 the profit margins of domestic auto makers started falling as imports penetrated 10% of the U.S. market for the first time. In 1972 U.S. oil production peaked and started a long term trend of decline, and in 1975 trade union representation of the private sector work force fell below 30% for the first time since in thirty years.

The straw that really broke the camel's back was the Arab oil embargo against the U.S. in retaliation for providing support to Israel during the October 1973 Yom Kippur war in the Middle East. The world price of oil nearly tripled over night, and gas lines became one of the iconic images of an unhappy period of "malaise" and "stagflation". In two years from 1972 to 1974, growth in the U.S. Economy imploded from 7.2% real growth to a -2.1% contraction. Inflation jumped from 3.4% in 1972 to 12.3% in 1974. Three days before the stock market crashed, Time Magazine had reported glowing economic predictions for 1973, but in the next two years the stock market lost 45% of its value.[90]

The recession of 1974-75 was, sharp, deep, and painful. It also signaled the end of a thirty year trend in the decline of federal government debt as a percentage of gross domestic product.

Under two Republican Presidents from 1980 until 1992 federal debt as a percentage of GDP increased almost every year, then leveled off and declined under a supposedly

---

[90] *Source:* U.S. Bureau of Economic Analysis Web: www.bea.gov .

spendthrift Democrat, and then shot up again under eight more years of "conservative" Republican rule. Who doesn't think politics is weird?

✧ 1981: The Fairy Tale Ends/Generation Busted Is Born ✧

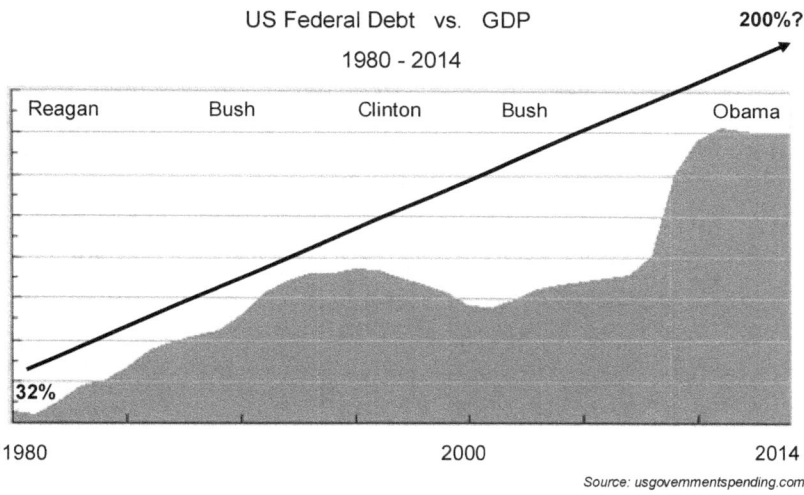

DEBT GOES OFF THE CHARTS: GENERATION BUSTED

The oil shock recession of 1974-75 was sharp but brief, and triggered more by oil prices than any sea change in the economy. The second oil shock of 1979 triggered the recession of 1980-81. This would be the ebb tide year that ended rising middle class prosperity in America. After 1981, for the first time in a generation, economic growth did not reduce the debt burden on the economy. After 1981 it was debt growth that fueled economic growth. We just didn't know it at the time.

✧ 1985: Back to the Future ✧

The "Happy Days" sitcom finally went off the air in 1984, but the very next year "Back to the Future" was released in movie theaters across the country. It quickly became the most successful movie of the year with a world wide gross of $380 million dollars.

By 1985 America was feeling good again, and a reprise of 1950's nostalgia wrapped up in Marty McFly's ripping, over the top guitar rendition of the rock-n-roll classic "Johnnie B. Good" ala Jimmy Hendrix punctuated America's change in mood from "What if I'm not good enough? What if they tell me I'm no good?" to one of hope and optimism. Two years later, on June 12th 1987 President Ronald Reagan stood in front of the Brandenburg Gate in Berlin and issued his now famous challenge: "Mr. Gorbachev, tear down this wall!" Twenty nine months later East and West Germans alike attacked the wall with their bare hands. The Soviet Union collapsed soon after that. America was back.

Ronald Reagan was derided on the left for his supposed lack of intellectual curiosity and simple minded views on world events. Liberal elites sniffed that the world was just too complex and too deeply interwoven for a 1950's throwback like Reagan to possibly comprehend. But what ever your political philosophy, there was nothing particularly new or revolutionary in President Reagan's choice of policy responses to get America's economy moving again. He simply went "Back to the Future" and used those policy tools that had actually been proven to work forty years earlier during the depression years of the 1930's. The two biggest of these were (1) tax cuts and (2) military spending. Price and wage controls implemented under President Nixon had already proven to be a failure, and the Carter Administration had already started the deregulation of the economy that was to continue under

Reagan. Carter had also initiated an increase in military spending after the Soviet Union invaded Afghanistan in 1979, but it was President Reagan who went big.

As stimulus packages go, nothing works to stimulate the economy like a massive increase in spending on a lot of shiny new military hardware built in a few key congressional districts. A word of caution and a proper perspective on the Reagan military build up is appropriate. During his farewell speech in 1961 President Eisenhower warned of the growing threat of undue influence on the government by the "Military-Industrial Complex." Earlier that year defense contractors had lobbied Congress to save the B-70 bomber, which the Air Force had cancelled. Congress then threatened to order the President to continue to spend money on the B-70 bomber even though the Air Force had determined that the concept was a failure. Recent advances in high altitude anti-aircraft missiles made the B-70 bomber a sitting duck. Congress finally backed down and the B-70 program died. [91]

(Flash forward - 2009 - Some members of Congress are threatening to order the Air Force to continue purchasing more F-22 Raptor stealth fighters beyond the 187 it has already ordered, even though it doesn't want them. Some things never change.)

At the time President Eisenhower made his cautionary speech on the growing political power of America's defense contractors, Defense spending was almost 11% of the total U.S. economy. Throughout the 1970's defense spending as a percentage of GDP had declined steadily and by 1979 defense spending had been cut in half relative to the size of the total economy.

---

[91] http://www.globalsecurity.org/wmd/systems/b-70-can.htm

So much for the threat of the military industrial complex:

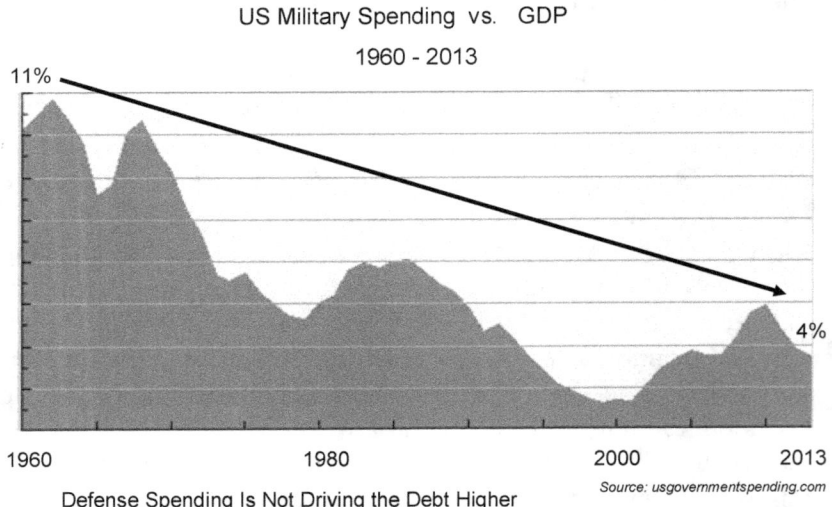

US Military Spending vs. GDP
1960 - 2013

Defense Spending Is Not Driving the Debt Higher

Source: usgovernmentspending.com

From this low point, Reagan's increase in defense spending was a fiscal stimulus to the economy, but was never anywhere near the relative levels of previous peaks in military spending programs. The general trend was lower defense spending as a percentage of GDP for more than thirty years, up until September 11, 2001.

The other big stimulus on the economy was the Reagan tax cut on the cost of capital, which greatly increased the productivity of investment. The Reagan tax cut on capital finally broke the ten year bear market in stocks, setting off a big run in stock prices that lasted for a decade. Reducing the cost of capital stimulates productivity improvement in the economy. Improvement in the productive capacity of the economy creates wealth.   It is the *only* thing that creates wealth. It is as fundamental as that.

Two other trends emerged in the mid 1980's that also helped make Reagan look like an economic genius. Oil started getting cheap again, and American auto makers started making money on cars again; to be more specific, minivans and light trucks.

Oh, and all those dire predictions made by the environmental visionaries of the 1970's? They simply disappeared. Just like the smog over Los Angeles. In 1980 there were 102 Stage One Smog Alerts in the Los Angeles basin. Almost every third day the air quality was so bad that children were told not to play outside. In 1990 there were 27. And the last Smog Alert in Los Angeles happened in 1997. There have been exactly... none since. My two children, born in Southern California in 1987 and 1992 don't even know what a smog alert is. [92]

Innovation and Productivity

The 1980's was an incredible decade of innovation and productivity growth. Smoke stack America was responding to significant competitive pressure from foreign manufacturers and the demands of the public to clean up the environment. Using less energy, becoming more efficient, and cleaning up the factories, it turned out, was good for productivity and profits.   An explosion in computer technology and the introduction of the first personal computers into the workplace was changing the way Americans collected and managed data, and marked the beginning of the information age.

---

[92] http://www.dailynexus.com/article.php?a=13747

By 1985 the voluntary export quotas on Japanese cars had been lifted, Lee Iacocca introduced the Dodge Caravan at Chrysler, which would remain the best selling mini-van for the next 25 years, and investment in environmental technology and energy efficiency had the happy coincidence of creating a new resurgence in the productivity of American manufacturing. Yup, America was back.

Unfortunately, not all the innovation that came out of the 1980's was necessarily received as productive or even positive. Deregulation of the economy had unleashed a new wave of productivity and creativity in many American industries, particularly trucking and the airlines, but the dislocations that resulted from corporate mergers, leveraged buyouts and industry consolidations led to a popular backlash against a perceived culture of excessive greed, as personified by the character of Gordon Gecko, the ruthless corporate raider portrayed in the 1987 movie *Wall Street*.

Only two years after America had celebrated its economic come back in "Back to the Future," Americans were beginning to question the social costs of the gut wrenching transformations occurring in the economy. Much of the change was necessary to adapt to a more competitive world. Some of it was just criminal enterprises masquerading as financial innovators.

There was ample evidence of financial chicanery that accompanied the necessary restructuring and rebuilding of the American economy, and there were plenty of anti-heroes. In March 1989, a federal grand jury indicted Michael Milken on 98 counts of racketeering and fraud. The indictment accused Milken of a litany of misconduct, including insider trading, and tax evasion. (Michael Milken was the ultimate baby boomer, born on the 4th of July, 1946, no less. He graduated Summa Cum Laude from Berkeley and received an MBA from the

Wharton School at the University of Pennsylvania, and became known on Wall Street as the King of Junk Bonds. He paid several hundred million dollars in fines and penalties and spent nearly three years in prison. His estimated net worth today is still on the order of *two billion* dollars.)[93]

Cooking the books became a high art by the late 80's and in a devastating collapse reminiscent of the financial crisis of 1929, half of the Savings and Loan institutions in the country went bankrupt, along with the FSLIC insurance fund that was created to protect depositors. The S&L business model of specializing in deposit savings accounts to fund home mortgages was already outdated and dying, and it was thought that deregulating these specialized institutions would allow them to innovate their way to profitability again. Unfortunately, many of them would just become a personal piggy bank for snake oil salesmen pumping bad real estate deals, or were just plain looted by insiders.

Texas was particularly hard hit. Half of the failed S&Ls were from Texas, pushing that state into recession. As bad land investments were auctioned off, real estate prices collapsed, office vacancy rose to 30%, and crude oil prices fell 50%. (This should sound vaguely familiar to you if you have been paying attention to recent events).

As it happens, not all deregulation turns out to be useful and productive. The S&L crisis of 1989-1990 ended up costing American taxpayers $124 billion dollars. We would learn this painful lesson all over again twenty years later when a handful of unregulated risk traders in the London office of AIG almost imploded the financial system of the entire planet.[94]

---

[93] http://www.forbes.com/lists/2007/10/07billionaires_Michael-Milken_SSM6.html
[94] http://www.fdic.gov/bank/historical/history/167_188.pdf

✧ 1994: Life is a Box of Chocolates ✧

By 1994 the economy had found a firm footing again following another sharp but thankfully brief recession in 1991. After a quick run up with the first Gulf War in 1991 oil prices declined to levels not seen since the 1960's and U.S. auto companies had found a profitable niche making light trucks, sport utility vehicles, and minivans.

In 1992 AM General, a supplier of military trucks for the U.S. Army, introduced the Hummer. Evidently some people were willing to pay a very substantial premium for a civilian version of a vehicle that could wade through rivers and climb mountains just to go to the grocery store to buy a gallon of milk. Who cared the gas mileage sucked? Gas was cheap again. Who cared it was uncomfortable to drive and ugly as sin? It was cool. It had to be cool. Arnold Schwarzenegger drove one. Forget the Japanese and their stupid small cars. Detroit metal was big again.

But simple nostalgia alone did not quite capture the mood of a less innocent and more sophisticated public this time. Times were good again, but America was a little less naïve now, and the country seemed ready to heal the worst of the wounds that still ached after decades of civil turmoil and upheaval. The movie Forrest Gump reprised forty years of the modern American experience, and through thick and thin, racism, hate, conspiracy, war, betrayal, abuse and discord, Forrest Gump remained uncorrupted and true to his simple truths and simple values of loyalty to family and friend. In the end, this man of limited intellectual capacity managed to offer redemption for all the sins of a generation. Forrest Gump made $677 million dollars and was nominated for 13 academy awards.

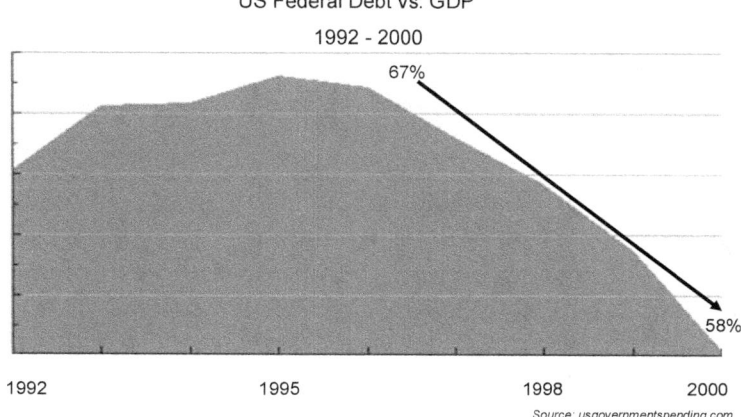

The Clinton Reprieve: Generation Busted Catches a Break

Bubble Six: Information Technology
Seattle, Washington 1995

On May 26, 1995 Bill Gates sent a confidential memo to the executive staff at Microsoft outlining his vision of the future being foretold by the recent emergence of new internet service providers such as Yahoo and AOL. In this memorandum he wrote: *"In the last twenty years we saw that exponential improvements in computer capabilities would make great software valuable....In the next 20 years the improvement in computer power will be outpaced by the exponential improvements in communications networks. The combination of these elements will have a fundamental impact on work, learning and play"....Now I assign the internet the highest level of importance...The internet is the single most important development to come along since the IBM PC was introduced in 1981... I think that virtually every PC will be used to connect to the internet...The internet is a tidal wave."*[95]

In this memorandum to his staff Gates went on to predict almost every major significant development in the internet for the next ten years: search engines, advertiser supported business models built around free content, file sharing, music, video, browser based gaming and communities, and social networking. Bill Gates predicted all of it. After all, who is going to argue with the richest man in the world?

---

[95] Gates, Bill - The Internet Tidal Wave. Microsoft, May 26, 1995. Made publicly available at United States Department of Justice. United States v. Microsoft Trial Exhibits

✧ 1996: Telecommunications Deregulation ✧

In 1996 the combination of dirt cheap and ridiculously fast computer chips, coupled to a modern telecommunications network, created an explosion in wealth producing innovation on a scale that exceeded all the productivity gains of the last one hundred years put together. The internet was bigger than coal, bigger than electricity, bigger than unions, bigger than manufacturing, bigger than anything ever seen on the planet, even nuclear weapons. The internet obliterated time and annihilated distance. For all millennia humanity had suffered at the tyranny of physical geography. Now humanity would live in a new place called *cyberspace*. Maybe Generation Busted would make it to the Promised Land after all.

In order to accommodate the coming revolution, Congress unleashed the innovative potential of America's investors and entrepreneurs with the Telecommunications Act of 1996. The Act both deregulated and created new regulations. Congress forced local telephone companies to share their lines with competitors if "the failure to provide access to such network elements would impair the ability of the telecommunications carrier seeking access to provide the services that it seeks to offer."[96]

This led to the creation of a new group of telephone companies, including one called WorldCom run by a guy named Bernie Ebbers. One of the unfortunate side effects of revolutionary periods of innovative growth is that there always seems to be some guy who thinks he is smarter than everybody else, who believes no one will notice that they are stealing the company blind, cooking the books, or both. When WorldCom filed for bankruptcy on July 21, 2002, after revelations of

---

[96] http://www.fcc.gov/telecom.html

accounting fraud on a massive scale, it was the largest bankruptcy filing in US history. [97] Bernie Ebbers was sentenced to 25 years in prison.

The WorldCom bankruptcy was even bigger than the failure of Enron which had not only imploded in spectacular fashion in another fraud scandal the previous year, but also took down one of the most respected public accounting firms with it: Arthur Anderson. Kenneth Lay, CEO at Enron displayed extremely bad manners by conveniently dying of a heart attack before he could be sent to prison. [98]

Who Needs Profits?

The Dot.com mania between 1995 until March of 2000 was as big and spectacular as any of the classic speculative bubbles in history. It had all the excitement and exuberance of the roaring 20's, when the real potential of an all electric economy was just beginning to seep into the consciousness of the American public. Just like electricity was before, the internet was a permanent game-changing phenomenon. Wealth and fortune was there for the having, and the world would never, ever be the same.

Anything with a dotcom suffix could get investment capital. Venture capitalists were almost in a state of panic that the opportunities to make fortunes on the scale of railroad barons and steel tycoons from the gilded age might pass them by. Business models with no revenues, no customers, and no profits beguiled investors with serious and straight-faced

---

[97] money.cnn.com/2002/07/19/news/worldcom_bankruptcy/
[98] www.washingtonpost.com/wp-dyn/content/article/2006/07/05/AR2006070500523.html - In fairness, Lay's conviction was vacated because the case was still in the appeals process when he died.

earnestness that profitability was old school. The new math was all about the burn rate; the rate at which the business model burned through the investor's cash.

The prize for the most spectacularly stupid dotcom business model by far must go to Pets.com - an idea for a dotcom business based solely on the premise that people would buy pet food on-line and pay to have it shipped to their homes simply "Because Pets Can't Drive."

Pets.com launched in August of 1998 and went from IPO to liquidation in only 268 days, after having burned through a whopping $300 million dollars of investor's capital. No independent market research indicated that any one really felt a great need to have dog food delivered to their front door via UPS. [99]

In its first year of operation the company spent almost $12 million dollars on advertising, including a Super Bowl commercial costing $1.2 million dollars. Total Sales? About 619,000 dollars. Pets.com lost money on nearly every sale because, even before the cost of advertising, it was selling merchandise for approximately one-third the price it paid to obtain the products.

Pets.com projected with a straight face that it would take 4-5 years and at least $300 million dollars in sales to break even in an industry with conventional profit margins of about two to four percent. But no one was willing to pay the true cost of shipping heavy bags of low value product through the most expensive distribution channel: express delivery shipments of one purchase at a time. The company was spending more and more money on advertising to lose more and more money on every sale.

---

[99] http://www.out-law.com/page-1143

On March 10, 2000 the speculative bubble in NASDAQ internet stocks peaked, and the party came to a crashing end. Just as fast as the bubble appeared it burst and disappeared. Over the next two and a half years the crash in dotcom stocks and technology companies wiped out $5 trillion dollars of stock holder wealth. But the internet lived on and the economy was transformed.

The survivors of the tech bust, such as Ebay and Amazon.com would grow into profitable internet business platforms. Email would replace the fax machine, and the pager would go the way of the Dodo. Google went public in 2004. Facebook was also created that year, YouTube was created in 2005. And something called the Portable Document Format, (PDF) first released by Adobe Systems in 1993 as a proprietary format was officially released as an open standard in 2008. It was published by the International Organization for Standardization as ISO 32000-1:2008.

Just like every speculative bubble before it, the dotcom bubble was a herald of dynamic transformative change in the underlying foundations of the economy and society. Speculative bubbles happen for organic reasons. They predict turmoil and upheaval, the collapse of the old and the dawn of the new. Like astronomers of old who trembled at the sight of the comet's tail streaking across the sky, you should tremble too, for a speculative bubble means change is coming.

Dejavu All Over Again

What is the point of this rehash of modern history? The point is that we have been here before; speculative bubbles, financial scandals, rogues and villains are organic to a dynamic economic system. They are a byproduct of the creativity and innovation that has produced the greatest wealth, the greatest productivity, the greatest opportunity, and the greatest positive change in the quality of life for ordinary people in the history of all organized civilization on the planet. They are unfortunately a necessary evil in a system that thrives on dynamic change to survive. The best we can hope for is to contain the damage when they pop up. Bankers call it systemic risk. You hear a lot about that these days.

✧ 1999: Party Like Its 1999 ✧

Every major speculative bubble in the last four hundred years of industrialization in the Western world has been the herald of some super-transformative change in the underlying structure of the economy. When a new transformative technology is first commercialized, world views change, paradigms shift, and once the full implications for the productive capacity of the economy start to be realized, the conditions for the genesis of a speculative bubble start to emerge, and the world is transformed.

Advances in navigation and ship building technology marked the emergence of an integrated world trade route over the oceans, and the world was transformed.

A real estate scam in a Louisiana swamp heralded the strategic importance of a new city and the emergence of a new continental people, who would come to define themselves not as Europeans, but as Americans, and the world was transformed.

Steam engines as big as houses had been used to pump water out of coal mines for a hundred years, then someone figured out how to make a portable, self propelled steam engine for use in overland transportation, and the world was transformed.

Engineers and tinkers figured out how to burn oil instead of coal in new powerful, lightweight internal combustion engines, and the world was transformed. Then they figured out how to send waves of energy through copper wire, and then through space itself, and the world was transformed.

We figured out how to wage war on a colossal scale, how to make anything we could dream up, make it cheap and a make a lot of it, and truck it, or ship it, or fly it anywhere on the planet. We could split the atom and fly to the moon, and the world was transformed.

And then we figured out how to connect anyone to everyone and anything to everywhere on the planet. And the world was not just transformed; it was reinvented, reconstructed, reconceived and reborn in the biggest, most colossal explosion of new productive potential more earth shattering than anything in the past four hundred years. It was *party time!*

The NASDAQ Technology Stock Bubble[100]
1994-2003

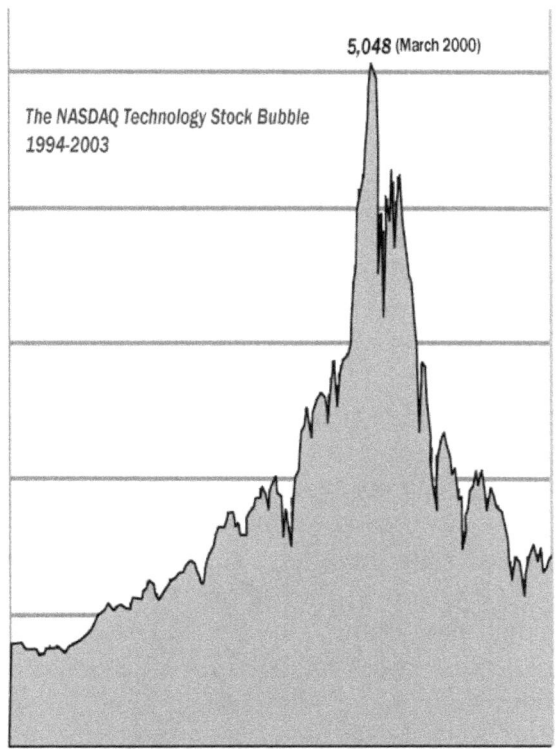

The technoloy-heavy NASDAQ Composite index peaked at 5,048 in March 2000 reflecting the high point of the dot-com bubble.Source: NASADAQ

Disintermediation

The Tulip bubble in Holland coincided with the first great age of globalization. The Mississippi Bubble of 1720 heralded the opening of the continental interior of the New World. The railroad bubble of the 1840's foretold the rise of a continental super power. The stock bubble of the 1920's

---

[100] The technology-heavy <u>NASDAQ</u> index peaked at 5,048 in March 2000, reflecting the high point of the dot-com bubble. Source: NASADAQ.

celebrated the arrival of the all-electric economy. In 1999, the internet bubble peaked, and then collapsed in the euphoria created by the infinite potential of the emerging information technologies. During the tech stock bubble, or what should more properly be called the great disintermediation bubble, the NASDAQ stock market index rocketed to a peak of over 5000 before losing 80% of its value over the next two years.

It you accept the premise that all the great speculative bubbles correlate with periods of rapid innovation and transformative leaps in productivity in the economy, then disintermediation is the grand daddy of all transformative leaps in productive capacity.

What is disintermediation? Disintermediation is simply the process of collapsing the supply chain and eliminating the middle-man between producer and consumer. In the "old days" commerce moved from raw material supplier to producer, then from wholesaler to retailer, before finally reaching the consumer. Every step of the supply chain added value to the product along the journey to the end user, and, by happy circumstance, this process added a lot of jobs and opportunities for employment along the way. Today, by virtue of the infinite connectivity and almost zero incremental cost of internet access, anyone can find anything, anywhere. Big box warehouse stores are a tangible example of disintermediation at work. Home Depot, Costco, Sam's Club are all warehouses that cater directly to the consumer. You can even buy a coffin at Costco. No one is safe from disintermediation. You don't need to go to a car dealer show room to buy a car. You can order it on line directly from the factory, including all of your options, color and upholstery.

The speed and pace of disintermediation in the economy accelerated the destruction of hierarchical and bureaucratic corporate structures all through the 1980's and

1990's and well into the 21st century. Information processing was getting so cheap and the speed of innovation was moving so fast that only the flattest and most responsive, and most innovative companies could stay competitive. This forced productivity gains and created new efficiencies in every sector of the economy that resulted in lower prices and a greater number of choices for consumers. Today, by the time you walk out of your local Wal-Mart and get back to your car, the information processing center in Benton, Arkansas has already uploaded and analyzed every purchase choice you made. The system is already predicting inventory changes across the distribution system, and is already preparing an automated replenishment order, not just for the warehouse to restock the shelves, but to the manufacturer as well, who is also monitoring the sales activity of their product in real time.

Disintermediation produced real gains in purchasing power for the average American consumer as the incremental cost of processing information plummeted to almost zero.

The internet didn't just eliminate intermediaries, the traditional brokers, dealers, and middle men between the producer and consumer; it annihilated geography, time and distance as well. As a freshly minted MBA in 1981 I worked laboriously with a green columnar pad and a pencil to create different iterations for a five year strategic business plan for a major U.S. Corporation planning an entry into Japan. It took three or four *days* to prepare one set of iterations. As an assistant controller in 1982 it took us *fourteen hours* to run a monthly trial balance of the general ledger on a main frame computer. Today that work would be done before I could finish typing this sentence.

Productivity didn't just grow quickly in the late 1980's and 1990's productivity growth went Super-Nova. It really *was* party time!

Disintermediation and the Rise of "Shadow Banking"

Unfortunately, disintermediation would later prove to have disastrous consequences for one particular industry: financial services, and the business of financial intermediation. For most of human history, ancient and modern, banking was a personal relationship business. The borrower and lender sat down face-to-face to strike a deal. Almost all loans were portfolio loans, meaning the banker kept the loan within the bank to own. The traditional banker was very careful in evaluating the credit worthiness of the borrower and the likelihood of default. After all, it was the bank's own money that was at risk if the loan failed. The process of originating loans to sell to strangers, where borrower and lender would never met each other, and where they shared only a tenuous connection through a loan broker that had no "skin in the game", who didn't really care if the loan could be repaid or not, vastly expanded the financial services sector of the economy.

It was also the beginning of the breakdown in prudent credit risk analysis. By the time the credit bubble collapsed in 2008 even the pretense of any meaningful underwriting criteria had been cast aside in the name of greater profits and greater commissions. The ultimate cause of the financial collapse was pure greed, unchecked, and unrestrained.

The first crack in the traditional commercial banking system, conservative, prudent and well regulated, was the popularization of the money market fund on Wall Street. In the 1970's these funds began to suck deposits out of the commercial banks and into wall street institutions that started acting like banks, but were not subject to the same regulations as banks. The term "shadow banking" would not come into vogue for another thirty years, but this is where the breakdown in the system started. For years, most auto loans, mortgages, boat loans, home equity loans, and equipment loans were made through commercial banks.

Unregulated "non-bank" financial institutions with huge appetites for securitized loans developed aggressive marketing campaigns that took most of the traditional portfolio loan products away from traditional commercial banks. Wall Street opened the door to a broader, more innovative and vastly expanded array of financial services and products, for both borrowers and lenders alike. Commercial banks, well regulated and conservatively run, could not hope to compete against unregulated Wall Street "shadow banks" whose real competitive advantage in gaining market share was really achieved by weakening the industry's credit standards, and in the end, proliferating debt to unqualified borrowers.

✧ 2000: Globalize Me ✧

America's greatest asset has always been its ability to respond with creativity and innovation to new existential threats and adapt to a changing competitive environment, even if it takes a few tries to get it right. One by one, every competitive advantage held by the U.S. economy over the last seventy years has been challenged.

U.S. car manufacturing dominance was threatened in the late 1960's by cheap Japanese cars, and then that dominance was destroyed by the public's growing perception that U.S. car companies couldn't make a decent small car. The Ford Pinto, introduced in 1970, became known as a death trap for the tendency of the gas tank to get punctured in rear end collisions and explode in dramatic fashion. 27 people died in Pinto fires, but in a production run of 2 million cars, that was actually probably about average for the cars of the time, but the damage had been done. Ford's image got a serious black eye.[101]

General Motor's Chevrolet Division also introduced a new small car in 1970; the Chevrolet Vega. It was completely new, innovative, and built in a state of the art factory with the most modern industrial robots available at the time. The Chevy Vega was named Car of the Year by Motor Trend Magazine in 1971.[102]

But, it had been rushed into production with a new state of the art aluminum engine. The new four cylinder sleeveless block weighed only 36 pounds and could produce 90 hp. It was a great innovation, but production problems with the new engine in the early model years tarnished its reputation with recalls and mechanical failures. Management also sped up the line at the Vega assembly plant in Lordstown Ohio to a miserable pace of 100 cars per hour to cut costs. This was twice the normal production volume, making it the fastest production line in the world. Labor relations broke down, and the cars coming off the line were riddled with fit and finish defects. The cars also became known as rust buckets, because of problems with the car body paint dipping process. Chevrolet's answer to the small Japanese car had left it with a black eye too.[103]

The Big Three eventually figured it out and found a new niche making minivans, light trucks, and SUV's where they could still make a vehicle of average quality and sell it for a profit. Actually, American cars are now the equal, or better, than any cars on the planet today. But I sure do love my Honda.

---

[101] http://www.conceptcarz.com/vehicle/z11819/Ford-Pinto.aspx
[102] http://en.wikipedia.org/wiki/Chevrolet_Vega
[103] http://www.conceptcarz.com/vehicle/z5211/Chevrolet-Vega.aspx

But something else happened along the way. America was becoming a less and less attractive place to manufacture goods. Overseas wages were cheaper. Foreign environmental regulations were more lax. The work force was more docile, (if not subject to outright repression) and had lower expectations for the workplace as well as reduced hopes for a better standard of living.

Making stuff was out. Finance was in. Manufacturing was out. Information technology, high tech industry and computers were in. Something new called outsourcing and globalization was transforming the American economy again, and this time it would take us to unheard of heights of prosperity and support another great wave of wealth building innovation… and then right over the edge of the cliff.

It was inevitable that eventually the U.S. would lose its total monopoly power in high value manufacturing as the rest of the world crawled out of the rubble of the Second World War. But it didn't really matter because as the world's economies recovered and grew larger the overall pie just got bigger for everyone. We would lose a few industries to foreign competition, but gain new markets for our own high tech goods. We could buy shoes from Bangladesh and sell Boeing jets to Brazil. We could buy televisions from South Korea, and washing machines made in Mexico, and sell nuclear reactors to India and pharmaceutical drugs, and wheat, and corn, and soybeans, and chicken, and beef to everyone else. And besides, we still had the best brand names in the world: Coca Cola, McDonald's, Levis, Marlborough, Gillette, and Buick, just to name a few.

Yes, I said Buick. In China the Buick name is one of the most popular and well respected car brands in the country. In 2009, General Motors sold four times as many Buicks in

China than sold in the United States. Buick will likely become a China-only brand, even as it slowly dies in the US.[104]

Globalization and free trade should have worked. And it did, for awhile. Until dislocations in the world financial system and imbalances in trade collided with super-leveraged hedge funds running highly sophisticated risk strategies that were fundamentally wrong.

Globalization and free trade is a great idea. Everybody gets to sell their stuff to everyone else and everyone gets rich doing what they do best. It is a good theory, if everyone is playing by the same rules. The OPEC countries get to pump cheap oil, the South Koreans get to build ships, the Chinese get to stock all of the shelves at Wal-Mart, and India, with an army of English speaking customer service personnel could become help desk to the whole world.

It really did seem like the right way to go. Going head-to-head with cheap foreign manufacturers became a race to the bottom for U.S. companies that actually made things. U.S. companies just couldn't get wages and costs low enough to compete with cheaper foreign made goods. Union representation in the work place started to fall, pension plans were cut, wages cut, and employer provided healthcare plans were scaled back or discarded completely.

After relying upon dominance in manufacturing and organized labor for fifty years of middle class prosperity, the model was starting to fall apart. Globalization would be the answer. Who needs a manufacturing economy anyway? We would become the great suppliers of creativity and innovation to the world. We would become the designers, the marketers, the innovators and the university educators to the world, and in

---

[104] http://www.insideline.com/buick/buick-is-alive-and-well-in-china.html

return the world would make our stuff for us. Factory work was out. Information work was in.

And our super sophisticated financial services industry would lead the world in risk management and capital allocation for the new global order. After all, despite the gutting our manufacturing economy had suffered in the last 30 years, we still had a comparative advantage in the best business schools and the finest universities in the world. We would produce the most highly evolved instrument of wealth creation on the planet: American educated MBA hedge fund managers and Wall Street investment bankers.

It is a great model for prosperity for the world. The mathematics behind this model of a super-prosperous fully integrated rationalized globalized and self actualized world economy is impeccable. It is elegant and flawless. If only it didn't rely on people to work. The math is perfect. The people are not. The most perfect mathematical model of the market devised still can not divine the mysteries of human psychology, or predict when or where fickle greed and fear will overtake each other.

Capital Asset Pricing Models

Modern economists, mathematicians, speculators, investment bankers, and money managers have been looking for the perfect asset pricing model ever since a few stock traders gathered under a buttonwood tree in lower Manhattan in 1792 to form what would become the New York Stock Exchange.

Whatever you are trading, all of the bid and all of the ask prices collectively accumulate all the information that everybody knows about the market. This should produce the clearing price of a trade, which is the most efficient price in the market at that particular point in time. But nobody's models work all of the time. Warren Buffet, the Oracle of Omaha, one of the most successful capitalists in all time, lost hundreds of millions of dollars in 2008 making bad investment choices. Bill Gates invested several tens of millions of dollars in a venture called Pacific Ethanol on the premise that you could make money shipping train loads of corn from the Midwest to make ethanol in California. The company went bankrupt. Even the mighty can't always beat the market.

In finance, trading, and all portfolio management, the goal has always been to squeeze out the most profit for the least amount of risk. A good asset pricing model should result in better decisions to both allocate capital to better uses and higher productivity and profits, and to serve as a restraint against too much risk and too much leverage. Anyway, that is how it is supposed to work.

The secret ingredient to making money on Wall Street is simple: OPM. It is called "Other People's Money. It's leverage. I can start with nothing and build up a fabulous fortune by using leverage and OPM. Leverage is basically borrowing money from someone with a low tolerance for risk and betting that money on a higher risk trade. If I can borrow money at 4% and trade it into something that makes 8%, I get to keep the difference. As long as you trust me, you are happy to lend me cheap money. As long as I keep making the right bets, I'll get rich and you'll still trust me.

Until I screw up. Then you will want all your money back at once, and then I'll have to sell all my bets to get the cash to pay you back. That's called a run on the bank. Then someone says, well if we can't trust that guy, maybe we shouldn't trust this other guy either, and that's called a financial panic. On the way up, leverage is the greatest wealth building multiplier in the universe. On the way down, it is a weapon of mass destruction that obliterates wealth in a flash.

Rise of the Quants

In the investment banking world leverage ratios of 10:1, that is, 10 dollars of borrowed money for every dollar of your own, were pretty common for a long time. Then along came the Quants. The Quants were a unique alien life form spawned in the bowels of the mathematics laboratories at the Massachusetts Institute of Technology.

These "Quants" constructed mathematical models to describe and predict the movements of prices in intricate and sophisticated detail, explaining the movements of interest rates, stock prices, the likelihood of bond defaults, the price of next year's coffee harvest in Ethiopia; and any and all manner of useful information for which you might think there is a need.

And now, with the advent of ultra fast computer processors and virtually unlimited internet bandwidth, the quants could run their models at the speed of light, and make billions of dollars on infinitesimally small variations in prices that were basically differences in mathematical rounding way past the decimal point. It became the ultimate low hanging fruit. All you needed was a pricing model and a computer and you could trade your way to fame and fortune. Even a mediocre investment banker could make a fortune, and the age of the hedge fund manager was born.

We Were Warned

In 1994 John Meriwether, another ultimate baby boomer, (born August 10, 1947, educated at Northwestern,

MBA from Chicago Graduate School of Business, former vice-chairman and head of bond trading at Salomon Brothers) started a hedge fund called Long Term Capital Management. The Board of Directors of LTCM included such illuminati as Myron Scholes and Robert C. Merton who would share the Nobel Prize in Economics in 1997. These were literally the smartest guys in the room.

In the first few years, armed with what proved to be extremely successful trading strategies, their quantitative model produced annualized returns of over 40% to their investors, even after subtracting their hefty management fees.

Unfortunately, the model they had built didn't include the possibility of a black swan event, an unexplainable sudden change in the herd mentality of the market, where all the sellers panic all at once and dive over the cliff, such as happened on black Monday, October 19, 1987. In a few hours of absolute panic, accelerated and magnified by glitches in the early versions of computerized program trading models, the stock market vaporized itself in a crisis of confidence. It happened then, and it could happen again. Their model did not foresee that possibility.

To earn its enormous profits LTCM needed enormous amounts of borrowed money to make the trading model work. And it did work, for a while. Then, in 1998 LTCM suddenly lost $4.6 billion in less than four months, and became a prime example of the risk potential in the hedge fund industry. The fund experienced a run on the bank as nervous investors started to pull out. Early in the year 2000 the fund folded, having proven once again that fundamentally, no one is smarter than the market forever and exceptional profits come with exceptional risk. The theories of Merton and Scholes took a public beating. In its annual reports, Merrill Lynch observed that mathematical risk models "may provide a greater sense of security than warranted; therefore, reliance on these models should be limited."

Eight years later Bank of America was brought in by the Federal Reserve to absorb Merrill Lynch, as it too imploded into oblivion following the housing market collapse in 2007 and the credit crisis in 2008. Merrill Lynch had taken huge bets on the housing market, and had relied greatly upon the exotic financial strategies it had previously warned against.

✧ 2001-2003: Securitize This! ✧

After the dotcom stock bubble broke in 2000, confidence in corporate America was shaken again when the full extent of the fraud scandals at Tyco, Enron, Worldcom, and other former darlings of Wall Street came to be fully realized. The economy was already slowing down when 19 Arab highjackers flew three commandeered jets in the World Trade Center and the Pentagon. A fourth jet crashed into the Pennsylvania countryside when passengers took up the battle cry *"let's roll!"*, and fought the terrorists for control of the aircraft, sparing the White House and the Capitol from destruction.

In response to these shocks to the economy the Federal Reserve started cutting interest rates. Between January 2001 and June of 2003 the Fed cut interest rates 14 times to try and halt the slide in the economy. The Fed dropped rates from 6.25 percent to 1.75 percent by the end of the year. Further rate cuts in 2002 and 2003 pushed down the Fed Funds rate in 2003 to a record low 1 percent, where it stayed for a year. Adjusted for inflation, the real cost of borrowing money actually was less than zero.

Housing sales and mortgage refinances took off. This unusually low interest rate policy also made exotic adjustable rate mortgage loans much more attractive to borrowers. Short term rates were ridiculously cheap. The traditional 30 year fixed rate mortgage where a buyer's payment would never change suddenly looked like a fossil relic from the Jurassic age of finance.   By 2004 more than 40% of all new mortgages being written were cheap adjustable rate mortgages.

And the debt bomb started ticking....

With super low interest rates and new loan products, housing prices looked cheap, and the economy took off. With home prices rising, people began using their homes as piggy banks. With a cheap home equity loan you could buy a new car, get a new boat, take a vacation, pay off your maxed-out credit cards, and then max them out again. The savings rate for Americans, already historically low, actually went negative. Why save money when you can print money with your own home?   The house flippers really went crazy. You could put down a deposit on a new condo project in Miami and sell it for a profit before the building even got built.

And the debt bomb kept ticking...

One of the least appreciated aspects of the housing bubble years, unappreciated by the borrowers at least, was the dramatic consequences of the shift from fixed rate mortgages to adjustable rate mortgages.   In a fixed rate mortgage the borrower's payment never changes until the loan is paid off. If interest rates go up, the lender eats it. The lender has two choices, sell the loan to somebody else at a loss, or accept a lower rate of return for the life of the loan.

In an adjustable rate mortgage, if interest rates go up, the lender gets to charge the borrower the new higher rate, and now the borrower has a choice to make. Make a bigger house payment, or pay off the loan, either by selling the house or refinancing the loan.

Of course, it works the other way too. In a fixed rate loan, if interest rates go down the borrower still has to make the same payment, and the lender gets a bonus. With an adjustable rate loan, if rates go down, the borrower gets a discount. The problem was that in 2003 interest rates were so low there was really only one direction they could go; and that was up.

Borrowers didn't care. They were getting great deals on houses that were only going to go up in price. Mortgage brokers didn't care. They were raking in millions of dollars in commissions getting borrowers qualified for houses they couldn't afford with teaser rates on adjustable loans. The lenders didn't care either. They were buying huge portfolios of mortgage loans packaged into bundles that the credit rating agencies all said were triple-A investment grade securities.

And the debt bomb kept ticking….

In July of 2004, after two and a half years of keeping interest rates artificially low, the Federal Reserve changed course and started raising interest rates again. And then it raised them again…, and again…, and then yet again. From the low of 1% the Fed would go on to raise interest rates 17 times over the next 24 months, finally stopping at 5.25% in 2006 when it became clear that the housing market was finally cooling off. But then it became clear that the housing market was not just starting to cool off, it was starting to collapse in a free fall. The Federal Reserve changed course, yet again, this time lowering rates all the way down to zero. The Federal Reserve took the U.S. economy, and the rest of the world with it, on an eight year roller coaster ride.

✧ 2004-2007: A Perfect Storm ✧

The cataclysmic convergence of historic trends, current events, unforeseen circumstances and unintended consequences that occurred in the first decade of this century was an incredibly improbable accident of history. Any one or two of the contributing factors might have resulted in a manageable disruption. The combination of all of them became a catastrophe of epic proportions.

Generations of future thesis writers will study this decade and wonder how we managed to turn the emergence of an era promising unprecedented global prosperity into such a tangled morass of incomprehensible stupidity.

The Global Savings Glut and the Emergence of China

"It doesn't matter if a cat is black or white, as long as it catches mice"

~Deng Xiaoping

China's road to modernity is a tale of woe and misery that spans two centuries. It has been a long march of cultural collapse, humiliation at the hands of colonial Europe, invasion and occupation by foreign powers, repression, subjugation, revolution, civil war, political paranoia, and government policy mistakes that killed millions by flood, famine and disease. The advent of modernity brought with it devastating consequences for the long suffering Chinese people.

After reunification of the country at the end of World War II under a communist government, a successive wave of centrally planned market interventions and suppression of private enterprise with heroic names like "The Great Leap

Forward" stifled economic growth for a generation. Five Year Plans to stimulate growth in heavy industry were a failure, collectivization of agriculture and anti-capitalist policies brought the country to the brink of starvation.

By the 1960's both Japan and Germany were enjoying new found prosperity, while China was gripped by a wave of political terror, which demanded absolute ideological purity to the socialist revolution during the Cultural Revolution. By the late 1970's the country was economically and politically exhausted. It had struggled for over one hundred years to find a form of government that could cope with modernity. The Imperial Order collapsed in 1911, then a Nationalist Republic collapsed in 1949, and the false promise of prosperity under the Communist People's Republic remained unfulfilled. More than a century of humiliation and misery lingered on.

Finally Deng Xiaoping, the new party leader, himself once a victim of the political purges, maneuvered himself into power and promised economic reform. While claiming that this was the new socialism, *as long as it catches mice,* the government abandoned communism in all but name only, freeing the economy, but keeping totalitarian control over the political process.

In 1980 the People's Republic of China opened a free market Special Economic Zone in the small fishing village of Shenzhen, just outlying Hong Kong in the Pearl River delta. From this humble experiment with free market policies Shenzhen grew into a city of 10 million people within 20 years. Since free market reform took hold in China, the rate of poverty has dropped from 53% in 1983 to 2.5% in 2005.[105]

---

[105], based on publicly available nominal GDP data published by the People's Republic of China and compiled by Hitotsubashi University (Japan) and confirmed by economic indicator statistics from the World Bank.

Make no mistake, China is still an authoritarian government that does not tolerate dissent and is pervasively corrupt, but in 25 years China has created several hundred million new middle class consumers, and they all want to buy stuff. They want cars, refrigerators, computers, cell phones, fast food, and air conditioning. China is now the world's second largest economy in the world and it *will* become the world's largest.

China is the center of the universe. The two ideographs that make up the name China literally mean "Center Kingdom". The Imperial Rulers of China claimed their authority to rule by a divine mandate from heaven. For a thousand years the world revolved around a Chinese sun. In the long view of world history, commercial, cultural, and global military hegemony by European powers and then the United States is a relatively new and potentially a short lived phenomenon.

For more than a thousand years the greatest empire in the world was on the continent of Asia. The center of gravity for culture, commerce and imperial power lay in the East. The center of gravity did not shift to the West until the advent of over the horizon celestial navigation and accurate time keeping devices made oceanic trade routes commercially viable.

Many of the world's great civilizations have mariner traditions going back 5,000 years or more, using seasonal trade winds, knowledge of wave patterns, or just the sight of land as a way to orient a ship in a general direction. But the ability to accurately plot a ship's speed through the water and accurately calculate its position on the earth, a true global positioning system, was not practicable until almost the 18th century, and it made England an empire.

Today, the wind is blowing from the East again. In the West, the year is 2010. In China the year is 4707. In the long view of history, China isn't emerging at all. After having endured a century of humiliation at the hands of foreign powers, the Center Kingdom is merely reclaiming its proper place under the mandate of heaven as the center of the world.

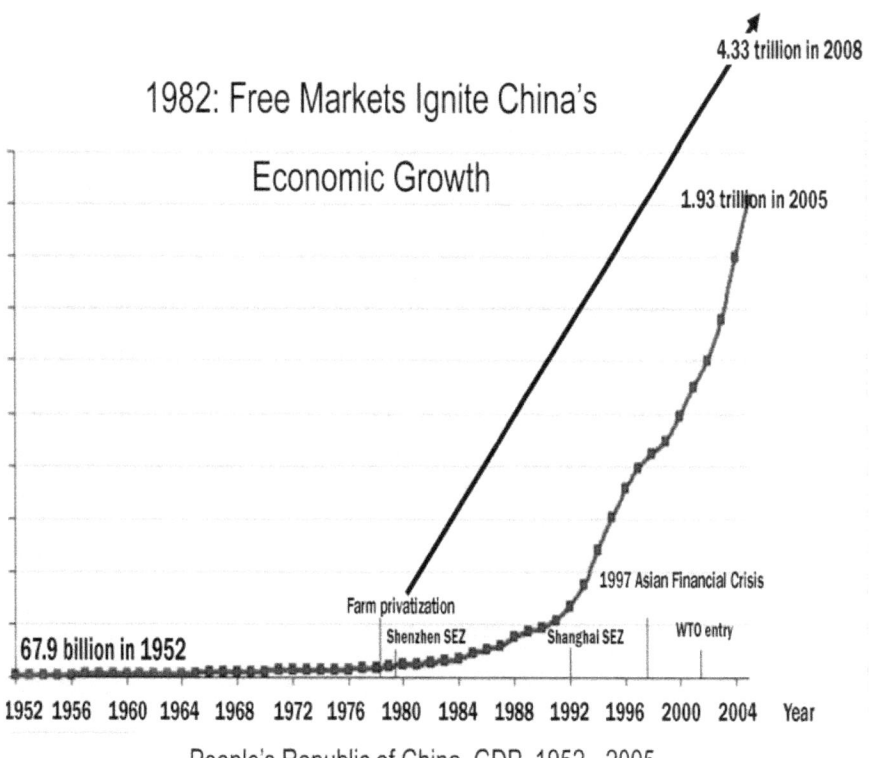

People's Republic of China GDP 1952 - 2005

The Rise of China[106]

So what does a resurgent China have to do with the housing bubble and the implosion of the U.S. financial system? The problem is savings. As much as all those new middle class Chinese consumers want to buy stuff, they also have a cultural abhorrence of borrowing money. They tend to save their money. We Americans don't. Robert J. Samuelson made the connection between too much saving in China and too little in the US in 2005, two years before the housing bubble blew up.[107] There was a lot of Chinese money, most of it U.S. Dollars actually, sloshing around the world looking for home. U.S. Mortgage backed securities looked like the perfect answer.

Stephen Roach, the Chief Economist for Morgan Stanley reported in an article written for Fortune Magazine in 2006, two years before the financial crisis blew up in our faces, that China was keeping about half of its gross domestic product, some 1.1 trillion dollars *per year* in savings. The personal savings rate in the U.S. actually went negative in 2005 as US consumers kept the party going by dipping into their inflated homes for more money to spend. The last time the US savings rate went negative was in 1933 at the bottom of the worst financial crisis in the history of the country. This time household savings went negative not to keep ourselves fed, but just to keep the party going a little while longer. Mr. Roach described the problem this way:

"There is a more insidious connection between the saving postures of China and the U.S.: Chinese savers are, in effect, subsidizing the spending binge of American consumers. In order to fuel its export-led economic growth, China has

---

[106] Ibid

[107] http://www.washingtonpost.com/wp-dyn/content/article/2005/04/26/AR2005042601394.html

decided to keep its currency relatively cheap and tightly pegged to the dollar. To do so, it must constantly recycle a large portion of its saving into dollar-denominated financial assets -- an investment strategy that helps keep U.S. interest rates low and an interest-rate-sensitive American housing market in a perpetual state of froth."

America was importing money by borrowing from the rest of the world at a totally unsustainable rate of *$3 billion* dollars per business day. Mr. Roach rather dryly described the situation as "Stressful," and with clarity warned that ""American consumers have mistaken bubble-like appreciation of their homes for saving."

The Real Estate Bubble

It would be the ultimate in chutzpah to claim that we went broke because the Chinese made us do it. But it is strangely ironic that middle class consumers in a presumptively socialist country save 30% of their personal income, because they feel they must rely upon themselves for their own welfare, while here in the bastion of free market capitalism consumers save absolutely nothing, with the firm belief that the government will provide for their social security, health care, and unemployment insurance should they suffer the indignity of unemployment. We have no one to blame but ourselves.[108]

Even with the glut of world savings depressing US interest rates and flooding the U.S. market with new money to lend and spend, the extreme bubble in housing prices that occurred following the recession of 2001 could not have happened without an accommodative Federal Reserve policy.

---

[108]

http://money.cnn.com/2006/03/03/news/international/chinasaving_fortune/

First, they lowered interest rates unrealistically low, luring unsuspecting home buyers into extremely risky adjustable rate mortgages at ridiculously low rates, and then strangled them with 17 rate increases in a row until the housing market finally crashed.

Chinese money was the gasoline, and a low interest rate fed policy was the match, but then things really got screwed up by the smartest people in the room, who should have known better, but could not resist the temptation to make rapacious profits on a model they knew was totally insane.

Risk-free Risk

In 1987 the financial gurus at Drexel Burnham Lambert Inc. came up with a new type of security for a client that happened to be a Savings & Loan institution called the CDO, or collateralized debt obligation. If the name Drexel isn't familiar to you, don't worry about it. They went bankrupt in 1990. Michael Milken made Drexel famous for his role in the junk bond scandal that prompted an investigation for possible racketeering charges by an up and coming United States Attorney by the name of Rudy Giuliani. Imperial Savings Association, the client that wanted the new security to help boost its yields, also went bust that year. I guess maybe we should have noticed that.

In any case, the CDO is nothing more than a basket of asset-backed debt obligations married up together to create one neat little bundle of risks and returns that can then be sold as a package to pension funds, insurance companies, and other institutional investors that need the highest quality portfolios with the highest possible yields at the lowest acceptable risk. Anything that has a tangible value as an asset can be used as collateral for the security. A mortgage on a hotel or shopping center, equipment loans for trucks and heavy equipment, car loans, home mortgages; almost anything that generates a revenue stream can be packaged up into a CDO. This was actually a very productive innovation that increased access to capital for a wide swath of solidly profitable companies at much reduced credit spreads, but that otherwise could not get an investment grade credit rating. It was innovative and made the economy more productive,

So far so good.

Investment bankers loved them, because they generated fees for issuing and managing the CDO and the investors loved them because they generated higher yields on their investment portfolios, in terms of the perceived risk. Many CDOs were rated AAA investment grade the by credit agencies, which in many cases was a basic requirement to find buyers for the securities.

The CDO evolved into one of the most useful and productive investment banking products ever invented. The theory, at least, is a good one. By combining a variety of different loans of varying degrees of risk, an ideal fixed income security could be created that minimized the risk of loss through diversification and maximized the profit to the investor. By putting less risky stuff with more risky stuff, the more risky stuff would earn a higher interest rate, and the less risky stuff would protect the investor from losing money. The model worked.

So far so good.

Then In 2001 a math wizard named David X. Li developed a pricing model for these new and very complicated financial instruments called the *Gaussian Copula Function* that allowed investment bankers and credit rating agencies to quickly derive the underlying value of any basket of securities. The math was elegant, the model worked, and overnight it became the standard pricing model on Wall Street and profits soared. [109]

Now Wall Street could bundle up hundreds of millions of dollars of home mortgages at a time and package them all up into neat little investment grade securities. Home mortgages are messy for investment bankers. There is no rhyme or reason to them. They are all priced differently, sold differently; they come in odd amounts with an unpredictable income stream. Some buyers pay down chunks of their mortgage early at random times for no apparent reason, or sell their house, or just quit making payments suddenly; too messy for Wall Street.

Remember Bill Gates and all that super fast computer software? Now you could take an impossibly complex mix of messy home mortgages and punch them through an elegant pricing model to determine with perfect correlation the expected rate of return on a huge bundle of loans, each of which was a different house, a different borrower, and a different type of loan.

Pension funds, insurance companies, portfolio managers and investment bankers all stood in line to buy them. They gobbled them up as fast as America's most unregulated and often times incompetent financial services providers, the home mortgage loan brokers, could write them up.

Unfortunately, the model was a gross oversimplification of reality and vastly underestimated the risk of an unexpected shock to the system, such as happened when the housing bubble collapsed in 2007. Investment bankers called upon Dr. Darrel Duffie, professor of finance at the

---

[109] http://www.wired.com/techbiz/it/magazine/17-03/wp_quant

Graduate School of Business at Stanford University to explain the real workings of the model to them. He warned them that the model was not a suitable model for risk management or valuation. Lecturers and finance experts of all kinds warned that the model did not allow for any unpredictability in the system, and it was dangerous. Warren Buffet warned that CDOs, rather than reducing risk through diversification, merely obscured the risk by making it impossible to analyze the quality of the under lying assets. Felix Salmon, writing for Wired Magazine described it this way:

"… People used the Gaussian copula model to convince themselves they didn't have any risk at all, when in fact they just didn't have any risk 99 percent of the time. The other 1 percent of the time they blew up. Those explosions may have been rare, but they could destroy all…"

But something called the Credit Default Swap made the pricing model irresistible. The Credit Default Swap is the cousin of the Collateralized Debt Obligation. A CDS is roughly equivalent to an insurance policy but not exactly. Insurance products and insurance companies are regulated, but a CDS is not. I can buy fire insurance to pay me if my house burns down. With a CDS I can buy a bet on the likelihood that your house burns down. You can't do that in the insurance business. It is not legal. But The CDS market is both unregulated insurance and not much different that a Las Vegas craps table.

Investors wanting protection against losses on their CDOs could buy for a small premium, a CDS that would pay them if their CDO went bad. Fortunes were made on Wall Street selling what investors thought was insurance against the possibility of losses on their portfolio. AIG, now infamous as the rogue institution that almost single handedly brought the modern world to the brink of financial collapse, created enormous profits for itself literally out of the thin air. Who cared about risk? The model said everything was copasetic and just in case, you could buy insurance too. The underlying flaw is that the model used to price credit default swaps had only been around a few years when housing prices always went up. There was nothing in the model to account for the possibility that housing prices might actually go down some day. Felix Salmon again:

> *"Bankers securitizing mortgages knew that their models were highly sensitive to house-price appreciation. If it ever turned negative on a national scale, a lot of bonds that had been rated triple-A, or risk-free... would blow up...*
> *"...Why didn't rating agencies build in some cushion for this sensitivity to a house-price-depreciation scenario? Because if they had, they would have never rated a single mortgage-backed CDO."*

Too many investment bankers who didn't understand the limits of the model were making too much money too fast to care. That is, until they had to pay up on all those CDS contracts they sold. This became the recipe for the worst financial disaster in history. Take a flood of new money pouring into U.S. financial markets from China, and combine it with a Federal Reserve monetary policy that, by design, was intended to spark a wave of mortgage refinancing and a real estate boom to stimulate the economy. Then add a new financial calculus that proved that risk didn't matter anymore, because all the risk in a security could be obfuscated with mathematical hocus-pocus that any credit agency would rate as investment grade. And then spice it up with some worthless default insurance, just to convince yourself you are a prudent asset manager. Now throw in the United States Congress and all the rest of it into the giant Wall Street food processor and hit puree.

This spectacular mess is now what is left of a substantial amount of the net worth of American families that took a decade to produce. The U.S. taxpayer bailed out AIG's obligations to the tune of $180 billion dollars when it all went bad. The worst part of it is, we had all the warning signs to stop it, but didn't learn from our earlier mistakes. There was plenty of evidence from the savings & loan debacle, the World Com bankruptcy, the Enron implosion, and the collapse of the real estate market in Japan ten years earlier. All the evidence was plain as day that unfettered deregulation could stimulate great innovation and be a powerful force for wealth creation, but with much greater risks if things got out of hand. And things did get completely out of hand.

Congress of the United States

The United States Congress was supposed to keep the lid on. It didn't. In all fairness to the Congress, the last twenty years has seen an explosion in new byzantine financial strategies and innovative investment products that were designed purposefully with the intent to avoid regulation and oversight. However, recent experience seems to support the proposition that not only was Congress lax in keeping abreast of the frenetic pace of change on Wall Street, it actually wanted to join the party, and may have helped create the sub prime mortgage disaster by encouraging lenders to lower credit approval standards. There is plenty of blame to go around.

Promoting home ownership has been a policy of the United States Congress for the past seventy years. The Federal National Mortgage Association (FNMA) was originally founded by the Congress as a government agency in 1938 to help keep liquidity in the home mortgage market and make home mortgages more widely available, and thus the American Dream of home ownership available to more families.

Over the next several decades, Congress would create an alphabet soup of different entities with different mandates to promote and expand home ownership. FNMA became known as Fannie Mae. Congress also created the Government National Mortgage Association, (GNMA) which came to be known as Ginnie Mae, to act as an insurer of mortgages, and also created the Federal Home Loan Mortgage Corporation (FHLMC) known as Freddie Mac as a competitor of Fannie Mae to ensure a robust secondary mortgage market.

Fannie Mae and Freddie Mac are unique in the world of financial intermediation. They became something between a private company and a government agency, something called a Government Sponsored Enterprise, or GSE. Their stocks are publicly traded on the New York Stock Exchange and they operated independently of government for the benefit of their shareholders, yet are implicitly backed by the government. This is a very strange animal, an ostensibly private for profit enterprise backed by the assumption of a government guarantee.

Fannie Mae was "privatized" in 1968 but it didn't take long before Congress and every successive White House Administration since, started tinkering with the model. For decades the back bone of the home loan mortgage market was the prime mortgage loan.

A "prime" mortgage loan is documented with strict underwriting guidelines. The borrower was expected to have good credit, the home was expected to be the borrower's primary residence, the borrower was expected to put down a fairly large percentage of the purchase price in cash with his own money, and the borrower's income and ability to pay had to be proven. Other debts, such as credit cards and car payments went into the mix.

In 1977 President Carter pushed for the Community Reinvestment Act to force lenders to make more loans in blighted inner cities and end the practice of red lining, which disqualified entire neighborhoods for home loans based on their primarily minority populations. To be effective, the traditional underwriting requirements for a home loan would have to be relaxed to allow lower income and less credit worthy borrowers to qualify for mortgage loans to make the policy work.

Every Congress and every President since has wrestled with the problem of how to turn people who can't afford a home into homeowners. The debate over which Congressman, which Act of Congress and which President bears responsibility for the collapse of the credit markets in 2008 is hotly debated and skewed by partisan rancor on both sides. The truth is that no one has clean hands in this mess. While Congress was tinkering with the mortgage markets and attempting to create ways to make affordable loans to people who couldn't afford them, investment bankers were using their new financial alchemy not just to tinker with the underwriting standards for the mortgage industry, but to toss them out completely.

Something new called the Alt-A loan made qualifying for a mortgage as easy as ordering a pizza over the telephone. Alt-A is short for "Alternative "A" Paper" which was supposedly as good as a Prime loan. The buyer was generally well qualified, had a high credit score, financial assets, and generally considered a good credit risk, but something in the underwriting requirement kicked the borrower out of the "Prime" lending category. Perhaps it was some one who was self employed and couldn't document all of their income, but otherwise looked good on paper. The Alt-A loan was the answer that unleashed a wave of new mortgage originations that allowed the borrower to "state" his income and assets without any documentation or proof.

Originally intended to be used for the most credit worthy borrowers, the Alt-A loans became a joke in the mortgage industry. They came to be known as "Liar's Loans" and turned pizza delivery men into mortgage broker mega stars. All you needed to make fat commissions brokering mortgages was a late night TV commercial, a toll free telephone number, and a telemarketing script. How easy is that? "Would you like to buy an $800,000 home on the salary of a third grade public school teacher? No problem, we can qualify you for that. Just sign this application here, and we'll fill in the rest for you".... (Insert a slight pause here for dramatic effect).... "Great news! Your loan application has been approved!"

When the housing market ran out of prime borrowers, and then ran out of Alt-A borrowers, the race to the bottom was on. Can't meet the underwriting requirements for a prime mortgage that proves your income and ability to repay your loan? No problem, if your credit score is good enough, just give us a wink, and we'll give you a "Liar's Loan."

What? You don't have good credit? You don't have a job either? Don't have any assets either? Well, ok, we don't really care about that. We have just the loan product for you; a sub prime loan. The mortgage industry invented the NINJA loan. "No income, No job, No Assets." It was both laughable and tragic. The joke in the industry became "If you can fog a mirror we can qualify you for a loan."

Any illusion of rationality in credit standards simply evaporated in a sea of cheap money, unsustainably low interest rates, and an astonishing degree of stupidity by just about everyone involved, but particularly the people who were supposed to know better: the investment bankers. They leveraged themselves 40 to 1 on the basis of a few mathematical correlations that depended entirely upon the heroic assumption that housing prices in the United States would never, ever, ever,….ever go down. Never mind that a similar real estate bubble in Japan in the late 1990's had wrecked the Japanese economy for a decade. That could never, ever, ever happen here. Home prices in the United States would always go up, always, right?

And then interest rates started rising. And then home prices stopped going up. And then the housing market stalled, and then it imploded, taking down borrowers, lenders, and several of Wall Street's most famous names. The Masters of the Universe were now masters of nothing more than the world's most colossal stinking pile of manure in the history of finance.

Alan Greenspan, chairman of the Federal Reserve during the housing bubble, was forced to admit that allowing the financial industry to regulate itself in the belief that free market mechanisms would restrain run-away risk-taking had been a failure. But the risks actually were well known and well publicized, but largely ignored by Congress, the White House, and the financial industry alike. In the witch's brew of lax oversight, easy lending and cheap money, the push to increase home ownership as a government policy simply went too far.

U.S. Subprime Lending Expanded Significantly 2004-2006

Sources: US Census Bureau, Harvard University. State of the Nation's Housing Report 2008

In fairness, several attempts to rein in the increasingly risky lending practices of Fannie Mae and the other big players were stifled by intense lobbying efforts against regulations to restrict the growth of the more risky lending practices. As early as 1999 the New York Times reported that "Fannie Mae is taking on significantly more risk, which may not pose any difficulties during flush economic times. But the government-subsidized corporation may run into trouble in an economic downturn, prompting a government rescue similar to that of the savings and loan industry in the 1980s." That sentiment proved to be prophetic.

By 2008, Fannie Mae and Freddie Mac owned over $5 trillion dollars in mortgage obligations on a capital base of $114 billion dollars, a leverage ratio of almost 45 to 1. When concerns arose regarding their ability to make good on their guarantees in the midst of the worst foreclosure crisis since the great depression, the government was forced to nationalize these ostensibly private companies at the taxpayer's expense.

✧✧✧

Bubble Seven: Financial Alchemy
London, England 2008

In the last few months of 2006, right as the real estate bubble was running out of steam, oil prices peaked near almost $80 a barrel, before falling to around $60 a barrel by the end of the year. Then in 2007 the price of oil started an almost vertical climb, setting new all time records without ever looking back. It hit $80, then $90, then broke $100, then $120 then $140 and then on July 11, 2008 oil prices rose to a new all time world record of $147.27 a barrel.[110]

In less than two years the cost of oil nearly tripled. In just nine years, the price of oil rose nearly *1000%*, that's one-thousand-percent, from around $15 dollars in 1999 to almost $150 a barrel in 2008. These prices blew completely off the chart. No one had ever seen $150 oil. What would that mean for the economy? This is a black swan event. This is not in the model. This changed everything. In a matter of mere months the price of oil rose to nearly *seven times* the historic average price of the last one hundred years. At these prices, the collapse of the economy was now inevitable.

---

[110] WTRG Economics. www.wtrg.com

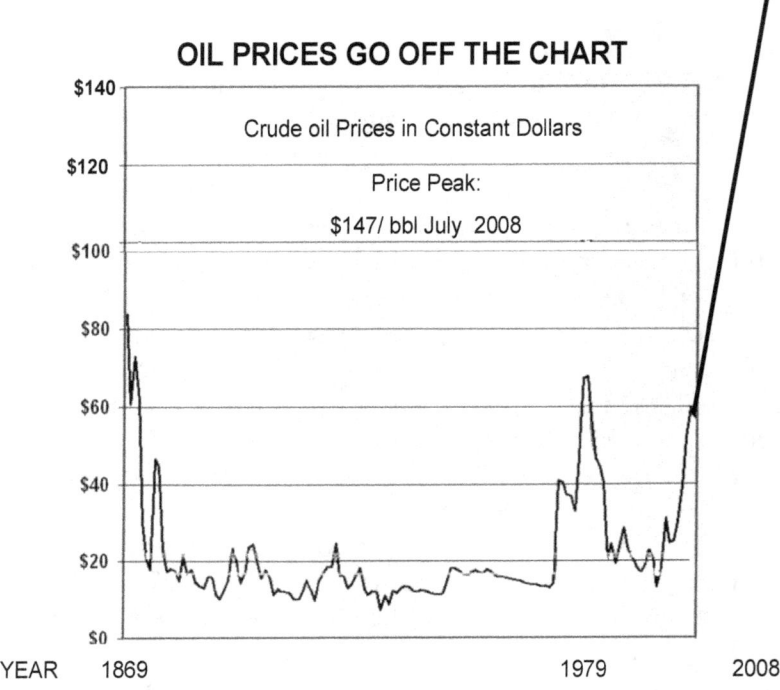

OIL PRICES GO OFF THE CHART

Crude oil Prices in Constant Dollars

Price Peak:

$147/ bbl July 2008

YEAR   1869   1979   2008

In the 140 year history of exploitation on a commercial scale, the average price of a barrel of oil has been remarkably constant, at around $22 a barrel in real dollar terms. Spikes in prices are almost always associated with wars, revolutions, policy mistakes, and political dislocations, rather than the underlying fundamental economics. Even as late as 1999 the world price of oil had dipped below the long term average price of oil. The 40 year period between 1930 and 1970 was exceptionally stable, even allowing for the price bump in World War Two. Then, in the last forty years, oil prices gyrated from peak to trough in wild price swings.

The oil price shock of 1973 was political fallout from the Arab-Israeli war in October of that year. The second oil price spike of 1979 coincided with the fall of the Shah of Iran, and the subsequent Iran-Iraq War. There was another mild bump in the price of oil during the first Gulf War in 1991, and a bump again in 2001 after 9/11 and a bump again in 2003 during the US invasion of Iraq, but through it all, the price of oil, for 140 years, has always trended back down to the long term economic price of about $22 a barrel in 2006 Dollars. In the last fifty years alone, the consumption of oil has increased in an almost vertical climb to more than 84 million barrels a day, but the long term price has always settled back down to the true economic price once a political crisis has passed.

The truth is oil is plentiful, cheap and relatively easy to produce. Any price greater than about $35 for a barrel of oil has more to do with politics than economics. From the peak in July 2008 oil prices fell back to this level within six months, before rising again to $60-$80. So what is the true economic price of a barrel of oil anyway? The answer is something called lifting cost. [111]

The problem with oil is not that it is scarce; the problem is that oil is ridiculously cheap to produce in a few areas of the world, and comparatively expensive to produce everywhere else. The lifting cost of a barrel of oil out of the sands of the Arabian Desert is about $2.50 a barrel. The lifting cost on an oil platform in the North Sea, or oil separated from Canadian tar sands, is about six times more expensive, around $15 a barrel. [112] This disparity in the cost of production has historically given Saudi Arabia and a handful of feudal theocracies enormous leverage to dictate the pace of technological change in the world's energy complex by flooding the market with cheap oil to undercut any threat to their position. There is no shortage of oil. There are vast

---

[111] http://www.manhattan-institute.org/html/_wsj-oil_oil.htm, *see also, Huber and Mills, (2005) "The Bottomless Well: The Twilight Of Fuel, The Virtue Of Waste, And Why We Will Never Run Out Of Energy,"*
[112] Ibid

deposits of hydrocarbons all over the planet. [113] There is just no reason to exploit them as long as there is still so much cheap stuff available.

What's Oil Got To Do With It?

You are probably asking yourself, what does oil have to do with the collapse of a hedge fund manager's risk trading model and the debt monster they unleashed upon the rest of us? The problem is this.

On December 7, 2005 Professor Kjell Aleklett of Uppsala University in Sweden testified before the House Subcommittee on Energy and Air Quality, outlining the prospects for a global crisis in energy supplies based on the premise that soon, as early as 2010, we will reach "Peak Oil": the absolute maximum of world oil production. It is true that we are depleting known oil reserves faster than we are finding new oil, but setting aside the question of "Peak Oil," global climate change, and the tsunami of new demand for oil coming out of Asia for a moment, Professor Aleklett, in testimony before a Subcommittee of the United States Congress made a startling public confession:

"Cheap oil made Sweden rich."

Sweden, that bastion of enlightened democratic socialism and state welfare; capitalism with all the sharp edges rounded off, became the third wealthiest country (per capita) in the world on a foundation of cheap and plentiful oil. It wasn't enlightened social welfare policies, or higher education, government regulation of markets, or inspired industrial policy,

---

[113] http://royaldutchshellplc.com/2007/10/31/fortune-magazine-oil-shale-may-finally-have-its-moment/

or even the royalties earned by the Swedish Bikini Team for appearing in beer commercials. It was oil.

Sweden emerged from World War II relatively unscathed, having maintained a somewhat strained neutrality policy throughout the war. Sweden escaped the ravages of combat on its own soil, but still, it was relatively poor. Post war, the rapid rise in living standards and income in Sweden was made possible by increases in energy consumption, which increased 7% per year, every year, for the next 25 years. 90% of the increase came from oil.

A respected Swedish professor at one of the oldest and most admired institutions in Europe made the most honest and straight forward assessment of the challenge ahead for us one could possibly make: cheap oil makes people rich.

Whatever else you believe about political philosophy, markets, regulation and social responsibility, or personal liberty, or global warming and the environment, (which I would be happy to debate with anyone on the merits as much as they like), the one inescapable fact of modern life is that cheap oil made broad middle class prosperity possible for literally *billions* of people. No country in the last 120 years has raised its standard of living without dramatically and permanently increasing the consumption of oil.

If we really are approaching "Peak Oil" we're screwed. If China, with 1/5th of the world's population demands access to 1/5th of the world's oil supplies, we're screwed. If global climate change really means we are going to have to move away from fossil fuels, we're screwed. Modern life as we have known it is not possible without plentiful supplies of cheap oil.

Something may be out there that is better, but it is not here yet. Oil is the essence of modernity. It is the only hard currency that really matters anymore. It is political dynamite and it is *casus beli*. America will go to war to protect open access to energy supplies. We've said so publicly and we've done so in practice.

Unless, of course, we can come up with something better. And we had better pray that something better is out there, or we had better start drilling like crazy. The safe bet would be to do both.

A Brave New World

Consider this. We are just now in the beginning phase of a transformation of our entire economy based on the never before proven hypothesis that it will be possible to increase economic productivity, expand employment, achieve economic growth, attain a higher quality of life, and do it all while increasing the cost of capital, raising taxes, and reducing the consumption of fossil fuels at the same time. It has never been done before. It is hubris on a galactic scale.

So far no one has figured out a technology to pack as much usable energy into such a convenient and portable form as a gallon of liquid hydrocarbon molecules, and produce a viable substitute for oil that is cost effective at the historical long term price of $22 dollars a barrel. That technology simply doesn't exist yet. Oh, and don't forget, we are also going to provide universal health care and pension benefits to all, raise the minimum wage, and reinstate a 19th century labor union model in the workplace that has been obsolete for forty years.

And one more thing, we are going to achieve all of this while the economy is staggering under an astronomical debt burden the likes of which we have not had to contend with since the worst days of the Second World War. Any one of these challenges alone would be a daunting task on the scale of an Apollo moon shot program. We are now going to try and do them all. God help us.

By now you know my view that speculative price bubbles are organic to our dynamic economic system, and that they serve to communicate predictive information about the future. Bubbles are kind of a collective subconscious sensory perception that reveals underlying truths, even if still dark and obscure. My best guess is, the astronomical speculative price bubble in the price of oil in the summer of 2008 was a massive and unequivocal warning signal.

Again, the long term average price of oil is about $22 dollars a barrel as measured in constant dollar value. The first oil shock in 1973 increased the price of oil by 200%, about double the long term price, and the economy went into a tail spin. During the second oil shock of 1979 oil prices spiked at 350% of the normal price, and we got inflation and recession at the same time, a period we now refer to as "stagflation." But nothing, not even two wars in the Middle East and mass murder on 9/11 comes close to the stunning *700%* increase in the price of oil above the long term average that occurred in the summer of 2008. This is a speculative price bubble on a magnitude many times greater than anything we have ever experienced in 140 years of modern oil exploitation. Whatever that price signal means, it must be something really, really big.

While the price of oil was soaring into the stratosphere during the early summer months of 2008 Congress held hearings to excoriate oil company executives on their obscene profits and wail against the evil speculators that were manipulating the oil market and demanding new regulations to curb their grip on the market. But not many people were asking what that ferocious price signal meant. When the price of oil trades at *six times* its economic value something is seriously wrong. Why would speculators bid up the price of oil to more than double the peak price of 1979 that crushed the economy and caused a deep recession then? Certainly not just for the thrill ride!

The answer may be that oil today is what gold used to be, a reliable safe place to store tangible, portable wealth. In 2008 trillions of dollars of supposedly investment grade bonds were suddenly looking like they were going to be worthless. Paper money was going to be worthless. Banks suddenly stopped trusting other banks, and it was a mad dash for the exits. The rush into oil was possibly not so much driven by the sudden urge to own oil as it was a flight of panic away from everything else. When everything else fails, the world still runs on oil. Oil is the only truly reliable and fungible reserve currency left in the world. And you can be sure about one thing. Every single barrel of oil that is produced *will* be consumed. Whether burned as transportation fuel, or used as raw ingredients in chemicals, fertilizers, plastics, medicines, or what ever else you can think of, oil is the most valuable and versatile organic compound on the planet. We should find a way to make peace with it, because it is not going away, and pretending you can create a wealthy society without oil is just a denial of basic, fundamental, organic chemistry, not to mention economics.

The oil price spike of 2008, which came *before* the collapse of Bear Stearns, *before* the collapse of Lehman Brothers and AIG, the banking takeovers, the stock market crash, the incredible expansion of the Federal Reserve balance sheet, and the biggest bailout of the banking system in history by the Treasury Department, was a gigantic warning signal. It predicts the potential for a catastrophic cycle of hyper inflation, government defaults and economic collapse. Hopefully, it was just a warning signal, and it will not come to pass.

In the years since the credit markets collapsed, the Federal Reserve and the Treasury have added trillions of dollars to the money supply and trillions of dollars to the national debt. This may yet prove to have been the right policy choice that staved off another great depression, but the unprecedented risk to our financial system and our economy is very real. The problem is, we have added so much debt to the system to stave off a depression that we now have a much reduced margin of error with which to deal with the looming bankruptcy of the Social Security trust fund and Medicare. We are going broke and the burden is going to fall mostly on those Americans born after 1980, who had very little to do with creating this mess. Generation Busted has every right to be really pissed off.

Wall Street

*"Double double, toil and trouble, fire burn
   and cauldron bubble"*
                    ~*Macbeth, William Shakespeare*

Great speculative bubbles used to occur once, or perhaps twice in a century, with a few hiccups along the way, and most of the hiccups were not really transformative bubbles in the true economic sense. Most were relatively minor panics or localized political disruptions, a scheme or a scam that eventually gets found out. The truly giant bubbles are few and far between, or at least they used to be. In the previous century we had one major transformative bubble, the stock market crash of 1929. We have already had three major bubbles in the first decade of the new century; three bubbles in eight years. The internet tidal wave broke with the dotcom bubble in 2000. The real estate bubble broke in 2007. And the oil price bubble broke in 2008. What the hell is going on? The simple answer is there is too much money in too few hands.

Do not misunderstand, I am not talking about income disparity between rich and poor, or the problematic concentration of wealth into a very small sliver of humanity, Nor am I advocating income redistribution or transfers of wealth from the rich to the poor. If you are looking for an advocate of social justice, I would recommend Mahatma Gandhi, Martin Luther King, or Nelson Mandela, but economics is a brutal truth. No one has yet been successful in making poor people rich by making rich people poor. Everyone who has tried it has only succeeded in producing poverty, tyranny, mass murder and famine.

What I mean by too much money in too few hands is a consequence of the incredible wealth explosion that has taken place around the world in just one generation. China created the world's second largest economy in the world in 25 years. India abandoned 30 years of state control over its economy in the 1980's and economic growth and living standards took off. India is now the world's fourth largest economy on a purchasing power parity basis. In the 1980's and 1990's free market reforms took root all over the world creating wealth at an unprecedented rate. Even the perennially dysfunctional economies of Africa started to show signs of life. Only the theocrats, sociopaths, kleptocracies, and hereditary autocrats got left behind.

All this wealth creation generated an enormous demand for financial management and investment banking services on a global scale. Money is skittish and fearful and greedy all at the same time. Money seeks a safe haven, and a lot of that money ended up in the hands of U.S. based investment bankers. And despite its meteoric rise in economic power, China is still developing its financial market mechanisms to manage all that wealth. The government is still authoritarian and corrupt, and the currency is not freely convertible. Not a good thing for an economy that is creating over a trillion dollars in new savings every year.

The truth is that the U.S. dollar is still the only game in town. (Or at least it was until 2008, the future remains to be seen). No one else has the markets, the sophistication, the depth of resources, the knowledge and the reserve strength of the full faith and credit of the world's richest economy to back them up. Enormous mountains of cash were ending up under the management of U.S. and London based investment bankers. And then stupidly, the top investment bankers in the world, firms like Bear Sterns, Lehman Brothers, Merrill Lynch, Morgan Stanley, and Goldman Sachs started stacking up all that money with astronomical leverage ratios. A conservatively run bank might have a leverage ratio of about 10 to 1, that is 10 dollars of borrowed money invested for every dollar of its own. These guys had racked up their leverage ratios to 40 to 1 by the time the house came tumbling down. Of the five investment bankers mentioned, three went bankrupt and the other two converted themselves into depository banks to qualify for federal bailout money.

When the market tanked, the over leveraged and over exposed banking houses fell like a house of cards. To prevent a total meltdown, the U.S. government stepped in to nationalize the worst banking failure in history. Free enterprise was the goose that laid the golden egg. The financial services industry, with a little help from the American consumer, created a conspiracy of greed that not only scrambled the golden egg but strangled the goose too.

✧ 2010: Tipping Point ✧

We are in the midst of something that is unprecedented in the history of the United States. Throughout our entire national history, the United States Government has used its debt capacity, the ability to borrow money, primarily as a strategic reserve with which to deal with existential threats to the survival of the Republic. Once the threat was passed the national debt was paid down.

Now, for the first time, we have used up our strategic reserve of debt capacity not to defeat an existential threat from the outside, but simply to socialize our mistakes and to maintain our standard of living. Milton Friedman in his seminal book on the causes of the depression of the 1930's blamed the Federal Reserve for deepening the economic crisis by sharply curtailing the money supply. But there is a huge difference between 1929 and 2009.

In 1929 federal debt was about 16% of the economy. Today federal debt is pushing 100% of GDP. If current trends continue, federal debt would rise to an astonishing 400% of GDP in the next few decades. This is a recipe for economic collapse.

In 1929 government spending on health care, retirement benefits and entitlement programs was virtually non existent. Today government funded retirement programs are consuming over 6% of GDP and the baby boomers are just now starting to retire. Today government spending on health care is 8% of GDP and still climbing.

What reserve credit capacity do we have left to deal with the next crisis? There is not much left with which to defend the nation in the case of another emergency, and the entitlement culture is making it worse by the day. We are maxed out for the next generation. Sorry, kids, when Gramps put that bumper sticker on his car that said "I am spending my children's inheritance," he meant it.

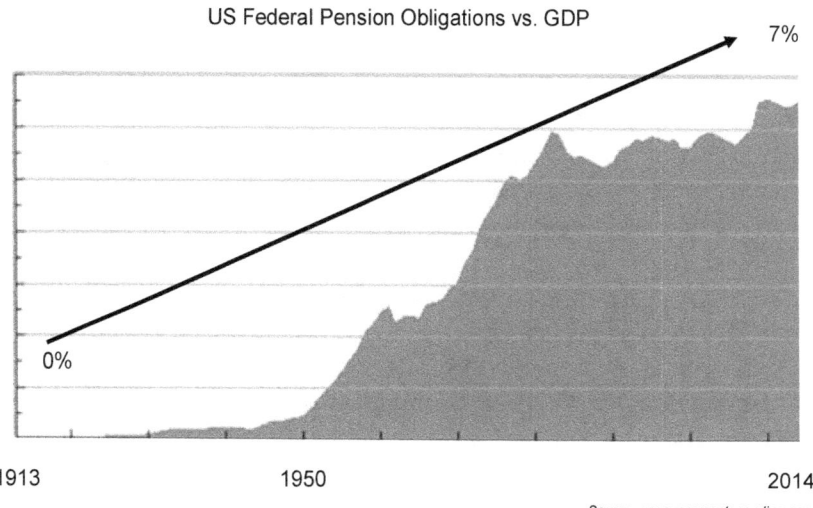

Baby Boomers Are Getting Ready to Crush The Budget

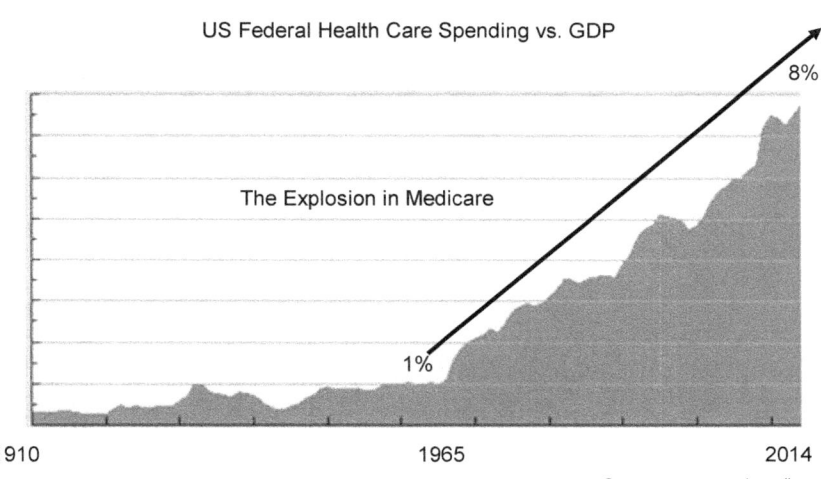

Generation Busted: The Young & Healthy Will Pay

In 1929 there was plenty of reserve debt capacity with which to absorb the shock of the financial crisis, but the Fed made it worse by constricting the money supply and the flow of credit just when it should have been easing credit and money. They zigged when they should have zagged and a manageable financial crisis became a full blown economic collapse. If we had known better, we could have avoided the worst of the depression. Ok, lesson learned.

In 2009 the probability of another great calamitous implosion of the economy greatly diminished with two years of back-to-back policy accommodation by the Federal Reserve on a massive scale. The Fed pumped in trillions of dollars in new money into the banking system and credit markets to prevent everything from going into gridlock. This probably was the correct policy response, but now the cupboard is bare. The Federal Reserve has put every stack of chips into the game. We had better hope for some really good cards on the flop, because we are *all-in*. Our credit reserves are gone.

It is not commonly thought of as a national strategic asset, but the reserve debt load capacity of our country in times of national emergency has protected the nation in every major existential crisis of the last 218 years. And once the crisis had passed the debt was either paid down or absorbed by a new wave of innovation and expansion in the productive potential of the nation.

From 1792 onward the debt load on the economy gradually declined, spiked briefly during the war of 1812 and then resumed its downward trend. By 1835, the opening of the Erie Canal and the emerging railroad industry vastly expanded the productive capacity of the economy and the entire national debt was actually paid down to zero. *Nada.*

The debt load on the economy spiked again during the civil war years of 1861-1865, and then gradually declined for the next 30 years, and by 1902 was less than 9% of GDP. The Mexican American War of 1846 and the Spanish American War of 1898 hardly even registered a blip.

The debt load spiked again during World War I, and then again during World War Two, peaking at 128% of GDP in 1946, before trending down again for another 30 years. In fact, the debt load on the economy kept falling even during the years of the Korean War and the War in Vietnam. The trend was a lighter and lighter debt load on the economy.

How is it possible that America could take on such heavy burdens and always emerge unscathed when all the world's previous great empires had collapsed under war debts? The debt load on the economy was simply absorbed by transformative innovation and an exponential expansion in the productive capacity of the national economy. America simply retooled, reinvented, innovated, and moved on. It is a testament to the truth of American Exceptionalism.

In the 1980's President Ronald Reagan seemed to have an instinctive understanding of the latent productive power of the U.S. economy to support a debt load that would bankrupt the Soviet Union and end the cold war. Whether by conscious deliberation or just as a by-product of circumstances, President Reagan used the reserve debt capacity of the U.S. economy as a strategic weapon in a tried and true American tradition. He would simply spend the enemy into oblivion.

Whether or not you believe this is not the point. Maybe it was the Soviet invasion of Afghanistan, the Polish workers in Gdansk, Reagan's military build up, or maybe it was just inevitable that the Soviet Union would collapse, but the illustration still holds. A reserve capacity to finance deficits is a national strategic asset with which to prosecute the will of the country in a time of crisis. Whatever the cause, the Soviet Union collapsed in 1991, and for the next ten years the debt load on the U.S. economy leveled off, and then started to decline, as it always had before.

And now, for the first time in the history of the Republic, our strategic reserve of debt load capacity has been depleted. We have used it all. Every previous spike in the debt load on the economy was a response to an existential threat to the nation that was followed by a period of rapid expansion in economic growth and exploitation of a vastly improved productive capacity that helped pay down the debt. This time, it is different.

We spent all the money we could borrow until the wheels fell off, and we now have nothing to show for it, except a really, really bad hangover. I hope you enjoyed the party, because now the bartender is bringing the bill, and it's a whopper.

✧ 2012: What do we do now? ✧

The short answer is to do what we always have done: retool, reinvent, innovate and move on. It is just going to be a lot more difficult this time, and most of the burden will fall upon the shoulders of Americans who aren't even old enough to vote. Unless, of course, by some miracle of divine intervention, the lobbyists for the AARP decide to spare the nation from the coming havoc the baby boomers are going to wreak upon the economy.

The AARP defines itself as "a nonprofit, nonpartisan membership organization for people age 50 and over ... dedicated to enhancing quality of life for all as we age." It serves a noble purpose, no doubt. But as 78 million baby boomer voters start to retire, the political clout of the old over the young is going to create societal rifts and generational tensions as the competition for scarce public resources intensifies, and their availability diminishes to pay off our debts.

The New American Aristocracy

We are now entering an era of a new American Aristocracy, one that will be defined by a struggle between the entitled and the un-entitled, as surely as was the struggle in the middle ages between bonded serf and lord. Aristocracy is defined as a form of government in which social class usually plays an important role in political and administrative affairs, where rule is established through an internal struggle over who has the most status and influence over society and internal relations.

If you are a baby boomer born before 1950, congratulations! You are a member of the entitled aristocracy and you will be relieved from paying off the nation's debts. If you are a civil service employee, transit employee, police officer, fire fighter, teacher or other public employee vested in a union retirement plan, congratulations! You too will be relieved from paying off the nation's debts. We hope you enjoy your social security retirement benefits, your pension benefits and your free health care. The rest of you out there, you are screwed.

Liz Pulliam Weston, a columnist for MSN Money says it this way: "The inescapable fact is that in 1950, there were 16 workers for every person receiving Social Security benefits. By 2015, there will be only three workers for each beneficiary. Fifteen years after that, the ratio will be down to 2.2 to 1."

Parents used to help their children get established in the early years of young adulthood and child rearing. Now the kids are going to be paying for their parent's retirement, while raising their own kids, saving for their own children's education, and all while trying to find a way to achieve their own financial security. Even worse, we are now in an economic environment, where for the first time ever, we are going to attempt a revolution in productivity and innovation by making energy less available and more expensive.

The Social Security Trust fund will start paying out more money than it takes in by 2017, and the Medicare Trust Fund is forecast to be completely insolvent by the year 2018. If the economy does not recover quickly, it will happen even sooner. Unless you are already entitled to your benefits, you are screwed. Don't get me wrong, Social Security and Medicare are worthy ambitions for a wealthy society, and in the end, we will still be a wealthy society. But there should be no underestimation of the scope of the challenge ahead. We have simply promised too much, to too many, to be sustained by the labors of too few. It is unsustainable and it will collapse if measures are not taken soon to reduce the coming burden that is going to fall on Generation Busted. Unless the generation of baby boomers now flooding the retirement system doesn't agree to a reasonable renegotiation of our basic social safety nets, they will surely bankrupt their children.

The choices are pretty straight forward. We can renege on our promises to everyone through outright default, hyper inflation and economic collapse, or we can recast the model and keep the wheels on the bus. Baby boomers were never big on delayed gratification, so the jury is still out on how heavy the burden Generation Busted will bear for a generation of hubris by their parents.

"We have met the enemy, and he is us"-Pogo, by Walt Kelly

PART THREE

Reclaiming American Prosperity

However we got here, we got here. But we can reclaim prosperity for a new American Century if we are willing to make the hard choices to save Generation Busted from their fate. These are our children. We owe it to them to try.

We are going to have to leave the financial wizardry and new math of Wall Street behind and reclaim American prosperity through some old fashioned basic building blocks of wealth and prosperity. A false sophistication led us to the brink of disaster. Now it is time for some basic realism and common sense to bring us back. We are going to have to rediscover the freedom to try, and the freedom to fail, without a government bailout for every failed business model and every failed labor contract. We may even have to consider rewriting some of our basic social contracts. We have to adapt, build, conserve, drill, educate, act with fiscal restraint, cope with global climate change, the health care crisis, and innovate our way out of this mess, and then just do it.

Adapt

In America the consumer is king, and the king is dead. Consumer spending in the US accounts for almost 70% of all economic activity. No one in the world spends money like an American consumer. Much of the economic growth in the past decade was fueled by distortions in the world financial markets that fueled not just a real estate bubble, but a consumption bubble stoked by a false sense of prosperity in those inflated home values.

Now, the well has gone dry and it is going to be a long walk to the next oasis. It is not much appreciated, but the truth is, the economy can fall a long, long way down without the support of the U.S. consumer. Millions of jobs and livelihoods in this country depend on discretionary purchases. These are the things people don't really need for the sustenance of body and soul, but would just like to enjoy. Trips to restaurants, visits to theme parks, cable TV, the latest in fashion, movies, clothes, cars, a lot of the "stuff" of the economy that keeps people working isn't really necessary for daily life.

I am sure the Real Housewives of Orange County will recoil in shock and horror, but most of the comforts of modern life can be done without before suffering any real deprivation. You need food. You need shelter. You need the love and comfort of a supportive family in hard times. You need to go to school. You do not need a $200 pair of sneakers. You do not need to have brunch at the St. Regis. You do not need a 60 inch plasma screen television and a home theater.

My advice to anyone who is in debt: If you don't need it don't buy it. It probably came from China anyway. Start with your most expensive credit card and pay it off. Then lock it away in a safe place. Then pay the next one off, but don't cancel your accounts, because what you want to establish is a strategic reserve of unused credit; unused credit capacity is the new money in the bank.

Buy down, pay less, and do without until you are completely free from consumer debt. If you have to make a choice between paying off your credit cards and making the mortgage on your house, pay off the credit cards first, and skip the house payments for a while. You'll probably be able to cut a deal with the bank anyway. [114] If you are tired, tapped out and ticked off, and if you don't like what your credit card company is doing to you, pay them off and get rid of them. If you are lucky enough to be in good shape financially, seriously look at buying a house with a 30 year fixed rate mortgage and shop for the cheapest rate and lock it in. That will be your hedge against the risk of hyper inflation. Interest rates can't go much lower, but they can go a lot higher. But don't buy a house unless you plan to stay in it for the next 7-10 years. You might not be able to sell it before then.

---

[114] Consult your own financial advisor before taking anyone's advice, including mine.

Build

The quickest way to pay down debt and rebuild our economy is growth. Nothing absorbs a debt burden faster than economic growth. We know that from history. But we have surpassed the sustainable limit of consumer spending in this country as an engine of economic growth, and we can't walk down that road again. Consumer spending absolutely should not lead a recovery this time. All it would do is increase our current account trade deficit and put more American money in the hands of the Chinese government and Middle Eastern theocrats who don't like us very much.

But we do have to find something else to take up the slack and create real jobs that will produce real personal income and generate tax revenues to sustain our economy while we get the debt burden paid down. Ironically, it is going to take some government spending to get it done, provided it is spent on productivity, and not handed out as employment protection payments to public sector employees unions or transfer payments to non-productive sectors of the economy.

We need a straight forward boot strap fiscal stimulus program that creates real jobs that generates real gains in economic productivity. Money spent on productive investments than can pay their way and produce long term positive results on economic activity. That means real projects that have real results, just like the Golden Gate Bridge in San Francisco, or the Hoover Dam in Nevada. Both of these depression era mega projects employed thousands of workers, and more than recovered their cost of construction through increased productivity in the economy.

From 1945 to 1960 spending on transportation infrastructure went up almost every year, doubling from a little more than 1% of GDP to almost 2.5% of GDP. Since 1960 spending on transportation has declined as a percent of GDP to about where it was in 1955, before construction started on the interstate highway system. The Interstate highway system was designed with a 50 year life span. It is now falling apart. On August 1st, 2007, the I-35 Bridge between Minneapolis and Saint Paul collapsed into the Mississippi River during the evening rush hour. Thirteen people were killed and 145 were injured. Time is up.

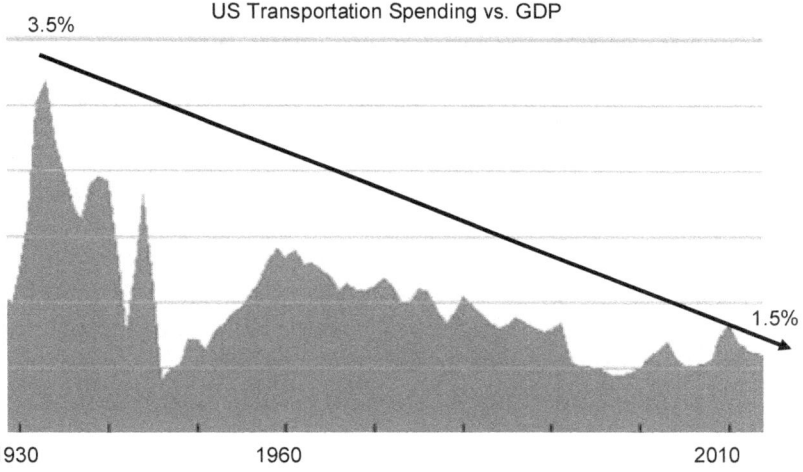

US Transportation Spending vs. GDP

3.5%

1.5%

1930   1960   2010

Source: usgovernmentspending.com

Social Spending Displaces Infrastructure Investments

The caveat is that stimulus projects have to be real. Not $300 million dollar bridges to nowhere, but projects that have a real, useful economic life of their own that pay their own way. Building transportation infrastructure has been a tried and true method of creating growth in the economy since the Erie Canal opened in 1820. New transportation infrastructure has proven multiplier effects, and can dramatically increase the productive capacity of the economy; railroads, airports, interstate highways, aids to navigation, locks & dams and port facilities all contributed to the development of the economy. Again, as long as the project is evaluated objectively and scored properly, and not some Congressman's personal boondoggle, it can make economic sense. New infrastructure investment can provide real jobs and real economic stimulus.

Transportation infrastructure built the United States into a continental nation and a world super power. We should stop apologizing for it and stop allowing our economy to be held hostage by NIMBY politics, fringe environmentalists, and radical anti-tax blowhards. It is time to face the truth. The economy functions on transportation. It requires public investment and tax dollars to build and maintain, and there is nothing more compatible with an appreciation for the environment than the jaw-dropping beauty of the American landscape as seen by a ten year old child from the window of a mini van while on the "Great American Family Road Trip."

In the 18th Century, rivers were the strategic gateways to transportation and economic growth. In the 19th century, it was railroads, steel and coal. In the 20th century, it was highways, oil, and automobiles. Now, the high ground is cyberspace and the internet. But for all the information and all the commerce that today changes hands at the speed of light over the digital information super-highway, it is still a guy in a truck, or a girl in a jet, or a loader on the dock that packs it, loads it, ships it and delivers it. There is whole lot of real world consumption that can never be replaced by the internet.

But more government spending you say? Remember, we have no reserve debt capacity left. If we want to prevent a hyper inflation and collapse of the currency, we must redirect money into productive assets and restrain spending at the same time. The only way to borrow more money for transportation is to spend less money on something else. Social spending will have to wait. If we redirected 1% of government spending as a percent of GDP to transportation we could alleviate 40 years of neglect to our roads, ports, bridges, and transit systems and put a whole lot of folks back to work.   The best social welfare program in the world is a job, and unemployed workers do not pay payroll taxes. We should be thinking big in infrastructure, as big and bold as the interstate highway system in 1955.

Conserve

The quickest way to rebuild the economy and pay down debt is conservation. The cheapest barrel of oil is the one you didn't buy. The countries of the Middle East, Iraq, Iran, Kuwait, and Saudi Arabia have the world's largest proven reserves of oil and the lowest lifting costs. That makes investment in alternative sources of energy risky and dangerous for the rest of the world. Any substantial investment that provides an alternative to cheap oil can be bankrupted. Ethanol, bio-diesel, algae, shale, whatever the source, developing alternative sources of energy on a substantial scale is hugely expensive, requiring billions of dollars to make a meaningful contribution to the energy needs of the economy. Any new technology to replace cheap oil will have to be competitive with oil not at $100 a barrel, an unrealistically high number, but with $35 a barrel oil, which is more like the true economic value for the real marginal demand of oil when all the political risk is factored out.

Any oil source with an economic cost of production that is higher than the last barrel of true marginal demand is vulnerable to an economic attack. All the Saudis would have to do is open the valves and flood the market for a year or two, and all the non-economic sources of production would be forced out of business. The only oil with a lifting cost lower than a barrel of Saudi oil is a barrel of Saudi oil that stays in the ground. Let's leave it there.

This is one debate that the environmental movement is right about. Roughly two-thirds of the oil consumed in the United States is burned for transportation. Getting more marginal productivity out of the millions of barrels of imported oil that is just burned up carting ourselves around would pay huge wealth building dividends in the economy. Yes, you really should check to see that the tires on your car are properly inflated.

Drill

We must use less oil; but having said that, we must also increase U.S. oil and gas production. Specifically, we must develop all the available oil and gas resources in Alaska, and on the Pacific continental shelf off the coast of California, in the Gulf of Mexico, off the Atlantic Coast, and all the oil shale in the Green River Basin in Colorado and Wyoming, and the resources of the Bakken Formation in Montana and North Dakota. This does not even include the vast new discoveries of shale gas that could displace millions of barrels of imported oil.

Wait a minute! Didn't I just get done explaining why we need to use less oil? That is not exactly true. We don't necessarily need to use less oil in the absolute sense. We need to get more economic value out of the oil we do use, and use it more efficiently. We need to displace imported oil that sucks money and jobs out of our economy and replace it with more domestic oil and gas production. We need the jobs, and we need to exploit the resources. The argument that increasing oil production in the US is pointless because we only have 3% of the world's proven reserves is just spurious. We don't really know what is recoverable, and the technology keeps getting better all the time.

But the real reason to increase oil and gas production is that it is the fastest way to relieve our level of indebtedness to the rest of the world, which is now a serious national security crisis that threatens our ability to direct our own will upon our own future.

America got rich feasting on the carcasses of bankrupt empires. We bought Louisiana from the Napoleonic Empire,

Florida from the Spanish Empire, Alaska from Imperial Russia, and in World War II we traded fifty obsolete destroyers left over from World War I for British possessions in the Caribbean. All of these now defunct empires were forced to sell assets to pay debts. Drastic times call for drastic measures. Every debtor knows that when your credit is gone you start selling assets. And then, when your currency is no good any more you become strictly a cash and carry customer. We need something of real tangible value with which to buy back all the trillions of dollars of U.S. Treasury bonds we sold to the world in the last two decades, particularly to the Chinese.

Inflation is traditionally defined as too much money chasing too few goods. But now it is too late to control the money supply; the Federal Reserve has been pumping trillions of dollars into the economy since the housing crash of 2007. The traditional role of the Federal Reserve was to maintain price stability through tight control of the money supply. The Fed abandoned that role when the economy tanked in 2007. Unfortunately, it was the best-worst policy response available. Letting the economy grind to a halt was not an option.

Printing all that money was arguably necessary to prevent the economy from a total free fall collapse, but the day of reckoning has not been avoided, it has only been deferred. All that debt has to be paid someday. Printing more money to pay it off won't work. That is called hyper inflation. The last time that happened in an industrialized economy the NAZI party came to power in Germany with disastrous consequences for the entire world.

We had better find something hard and tangible to back up all that paper money, or we risk a long serious bout of hyper inflation and economic distress. Money used to be backed by gold. But for all you gold bugs out there, I will have to disappoint you. The supply of gold is just too finite to accommodate the modern world and the enormous expansion of wealth in just the last generation. Faith in the gold standard is just a romantic anachronism, a sentimental nostalgia for a world view that can't deal with modernity.

But it is also true that a currency has to be backed by something tangible. America's unassailable economic preeminence used to be enough to back the currency, but now our credibility is tarnished around the world and we need something tangible to back up the Dollar again. It used to be gold. Today, currency is backed by oil. It is the one form of portable, tangible wealth that every country in the world holding U.S. Dollars would be willing to trade for. China is a patient country with a very long view of history. If they know we will sell them Alaskan oil to buy back our debt, they will probably be willing to continue holding U.S. Treasury Bonds & U.S. Dollar reserves.

Raise taxes on gas if you must, tax carbon if you must, and by all means, improve the fuel efficiency standards of cars and light trucks, retool for hybrids and natural gas powered tucks, all of which would be good for national security. But the fact is we are a debtor nation and we need to sell some hard assets to pay off our debts.

Increasing oil and gas production in California and Alaska and selling it to the Chinese would allow us to retire our national debt in an orderly fashion, strengthen the U.S. Dollar, create American jobs and stimulate the economy, which in California is now totally in the tank.

There is another strategic benefit to vastly expanding U.S. production while making gains in conservation and curtailing imports at the same time. Expansion in U.S. oil and gas production, coupled with conservation gains, would break the strategic lock that Saudi Arabia has on the ability to manipulate the price of oil by ramping up or choking off production.

The Federal Reserve Bank's most important mission, above all else, is to conduct monetary policy to achieve price stability in the economy. It is just as important to the survival of the U.S. economy to achieve some level of predictability in the price of oil. There is no underlying economic basis for the price swings of 2008, where oil reached a high over $140 dollars a barrel before crashing to around $30. The United States has a strategic petroleum reserve of millions of barrels of oil stuffed into salt caverns. What we also need is a strategic reserve in production capacity as well. Relatively small changes would have huge positive impacts. Small changes at the margins of demand can have huge impacts in the equilibrium price of a commodity. A 10% drop in oil imports coupled with a 10% increase in U.S. oil production and a 10% reduction in demand through improvements in efficiency and energy conservation would vastly alter the strategic equation for energy and national security. It would greatly reduce our vulnerability to another economic meltdown caused by $4 a gallon gasoline.

We should engage in a surge of natural gas and oil production, export as much as we can to the rest of the world, and buy back our foreign held debt. Once a reasonable debt payment plan is worked out with the Chinese and the debt load burden on the economy falls to a sustainable level, cap the wells and maintain them as part of the Strategic Petroleum Reserve to be used in times of national emergency.

Or, we could always do what defunct empires have done in the past, have an asset sale. Maybe we could get a good price for Guam... or Hawaii for that matter. Actually, let's sell them Texas. Those people still think of themselves as a separate country anyway. Their own Governor even recently threatened to secede from the Union! ….Again! Good riddance, I say. Ok. I'm just kidding; we would never sell the Dallas Cowboys' Cheerleaders. The Chinese can have Las Vegas instead. Maybe we could win some of our money back.

What about the environmental consequences of oil drilling in environmentally sensitive habitats? I can guarantee you, the environmental consequences of a collapse of the Dollar and the economic dislocations of hyperinflation would by far be more devastating to the environment than drilling for oil with today's technologies. Wealthy people care about the environment. Poor people care about survival. I'll even meet the environmental movement half way. For every barrel of new U.S. production put on the market and sold to the Chinese, we reduce our imports of oil by the same amount through conservation programs and efficiency improvements. That would at least make the oil-for-debt payment plan carbon neutral.

It would sure be a better solution than taking America to the pawn shop, because that is the alternative. That is where debtors with no credit go to get money to keep body and soul together, to the pawn shop.

Entitlement Reform

If you want a true lesson in economics, just ask any employer what it costs per labor hour to run their business, whether it is making a product or providing a service. Any true business manager will be able to tell you to the penny how much his employees cost on an hourly basis, and how much value that employee produces for the business for that one hour of labor. Then repeat that exercise, and ask the employees of that business how much they make per hour. You might be amazed at how far apart those two numbers are.

Invariably, at every business I have run, big or small, there came a day when I had to explain to an employee the difference between what they earned versus what they actually cost the business. This is a conversation that typically occurs after a performance review with an employee who is working at a satisfactory level of proficiency in their job, with few or no discipline problems, but gets no raise.

(Sidebar: Seniority by itself has no economic value. Are more experienced employees more productive? Usually. Are older workers more stable, and less likely to have attendance problems, or turn over less often? Probably. Does seniority provide some intangible sense of fairness in the workplace that might make some contribution to morale and overall productivity? Maybe, and then again maybe not).

I'll say it again. Seniority by itself has no economic value at all. The fact that you have been doing a job longer than someone else does not create any additional value to your employer. If you are in a union contract or some other arrangement where your compensation is tied to your time in grade, you are an economic fossil and subject to extinction. In the airline and auto manufacturing industries, we call these "Legacy Costs." Your employer will declare bankruptcy to get rid of you. Or, your job will be outsourced to a cheaper labor market, or your factory will close and relocate to a lower cost country.

I find there is usually a large perception gap between what employees think they make and what they actually cost the business where they work. The conversation usually goes something like "I only make $17 an hour, so if I am doing a good job why can't I have a raise?" The answer goes like this: "You make $17 an hour, but you cost $23 dollars an hour." This is usually followed by a bewildered silence and a then a quizzical look, as if to say "Boy, what I could do with $23 dollars an hour!"

And if you think union employees are better represented in the work place than non-union employees, perhaps that may have been true in the past. But what good is your union benefit package if your pension fund is bankrupt and your healthcare is cancelled?

The economic reality is that a job that cannot produce more value to the company than it costs is a job that is on the endangered species list. About the only jobs immune from economic realities are government employee unions.

Government is the ultimate monopoly. You can't outsource it. Well, actually you can, at least some of its services. Government uses third party contractors to provide services all the time. Eventually, as the debt load increases, and tax burdens go up to pay off all that borrowed money, the pressure will even reach into the halls of government, and the pressure will increase to cut pay and benefits, and when the unions resist, their services will finally be outsourced to a cheaper private party contractor.

Fiscal Restraint - Social Insecurity

Getting to the point now, why is there such a great gap between what employers know their employees actually cost and what employees think they make? The answer is employer payroll taxes. Unemployment goes down when the cost to the employer for the employee's wages and benefits is less than the value the employee creates by doing the job. In plain English, if your employer can't make any money off of you, she doesn't need you, and won't keep you.

Does that make you feel like a member of the alienated proletariat? Exploited by the dark forces of capitalist greed? Fine, then go out and start your own business. Then you will really be in for a shock, when you, by yourself, have to pay both the employee and employer contributions for payroll taxes.

You are free to believe whatever you want. All workers should receive a living wage; all workers should have an employer provided healthcare plan; all people everywhere should live in dignity and enjoy a meaningful quality of life. It is a wonderful aspiration to have. And everyone should receive guaranteed social security income at age 65.

Let's have a show of hands: raise your hand if you know what is a defined benefit pension? Defined benefit pensions are a thing of the past. If you have one, consider yourself a member of the new American Aristocracy. If you are under the age of thirty, there is a good chance you don't even know what a defined benefit pension is. Ask your mother or grandfather about it. He might even tell you about the "good old days" when you could actually spend a career working at the same company and not worry that the company would leave town to lower its production costs in order to survive.

Global Climate Change

In the language of economics, global climate change is the ultimate externality. It would be dishonest to promote expanding oil production and consumption of fossil fuels without addressing this issue. Global climate change is a reality.

Climatologists have correlated the historical data pretty accurately. Carbon in the atmosphere goes up, and the Earth is warmed. Carbon in the atmosphere goes down, and the Earth is cooled. So, the debate about whether global warming of the earth can be caused by human activity pumping carbon dioxide into the atmosphere is pretty much a decided issue, except we don't really know for sure if all the hysteria around the science is warranted or not, and we don't really know for sure if it will be manageable or not. It probably should be received with a dose of skepticism and caution. For all we know the next volcanic eruption somewhere could spew enough sulfur into the atmosphere to cause massive crop failures and famines due to prolonged global cooling. We just don't know.

There is no question however, that the environmental crisis of the 1970's was a real and present danger to the health and well being of humanity. But the population bomb did not outstrip the earth's carrying capacity, and if anything, rising standards of living around the world have done more to promote conservation and interest in the environment, not less. Famine and environmental degradation today have much more to do with political dislocations and civil war than any real threat to our capacity to feed, clothe, shelter ourselves, and provide ourselves with clean air to breathe and clean water to drink. But hey, if you think that living in an unheated barn in the Vermont countryside where you can express yourself on a foot powered potter's wheel makes you a morally superior being, well then, have at it. But it doesn't make the world a better place.

On the other hand, it is absolutely true that the actual cost of burning fossil fuels is higher than is reflected in the market price, because there is no cost for dumping the byproducts of fossil fuel combustion into the world's largest sink hole, the air we breathe. So here lies the dilemma: No one has yet figured out how to improve the quality of life and standard of living of subsistence level farmers without dramatically increasing their access to and consumption of fossil fuels. Subsistence level farmers slash and burn to survive. A farmer with an advanced quality of life uses GPS navigation technology and laser imaging to husband the soil; level the fields, conserve water, and monitor pests. Her goal is to minimize the production inputs and maximize production output.

A subsistence level farmer uses a machete and a match. The Amazon rain forest is one of the greatest carbon sinks on the planet. If you want to reduce the amount of rain forest that is lost to slash and burn farming, you might want to give the subsistence level farmer lots of oil to burn instead of burning virgin rain forest. It might do a lot less damage to the environment in the long run.

If you think about it, thirty years ago, the Malthusians were predicting that today we would all be wearing gas masks and living desperate lives in a post apocalyptic world devastated by global famine and complete collapse of the biosphere. None of that happened. And by historical standards, oil is very clean fuel.

Prior to the advent of cheap internal combustion engines the world's major cities were choked with the feces, urine, and the carcasses of dead animals. Before natural gas and electricity became common place for home cooking and heating, a poisonous soup of fog and coal smoke wafted through major cities at levels of toxicity we would never tolerate today. And no one even talks about the hole in the ozone layer anymore.

So, if today our biggest problem is a pollutant that is colorless, odorless, and completely non-toxic, I would say we have done pretty well in a very short time. The challenge we face is that every available alternative to oil is more expensive and more intrusive upon the environment than carbon dioxide.

Don't like CO2? Then are you willing to have a nuclear power plant in your backyard? Are you willing to live within the flutter zone of a wind turbine that kills bats and song birds and emits annoying low frequency noise pollution? Are you willing to trade the survival of an exotic minnow for cheap and abundant hydroelectric power? Are you willing to drive a less crash worthy car? Are you willing to put solar panels on the roof of your house at three times the price to light and heat your home? For my sake, I hope so. I am hoping you make that choice; because then I won't have to.

Seriously, by all means, let's conserve. Let's improve energy efficiency. Let's invent new technologies and commercialize new processes. But let's stop demonizing conventional oil as the environmental boogeyman. We could do a lot worse, and we do. Just do the math. Figure out the cost of inputs in, the costs of outputs out, compensate for the known externalities, and go with what works. Let's set politics and ideology aside and do a straight up side by side comparison of the merits of the best commercially available technology and evaluate the value of the fuel produced and adjust it for the environmental costs. Let's look at three options:

(1) Conventional fuel in a conventional internal combustion engine. (2) Gas-electric hybrids powered by nickel-metal-hydride batteries, and (3) conventional engines powered by renewable corn based ethanol.

By the time this book hits print you will be reading about the 2010 Volkswagen Polo, powered by an ultra clean 1.2 liter turbocharged BlueMotion diesel engine. It will get nearly 70 mpg on ultra low sulfur diesel fuel. You do not need to produce exotic batteries with toxic metals and a downstream waste problem to dramatically improve the energy efficiency of your car. You can drive one of these, or one of its competitors. Think this is something new and exotic? Not really. The Europeans have been driving zippy little diesel powered cars for years. We might be driving them too, if the auto manufacturers had not given diesel fuel and diesel engines a black eye back in the 1970s by trying to cram obsolete diesel engines designed for trucks into passengers cars. They were smoky, noisy, and balky and Americans hated them. But now it is time for a new look at diesel engine technology.

Fuels

Let's evaluate conventional gasoline, diesel fuel, and ethanol. Not all fuel is the same. Ethanol has only 2/3 the energy content of gasoline, and only a little more than 50% of the energy content of conventional diesel fuel. Energy content is measured in British Thermal Units, or BTUs. A gallon of Ethanol contains about 76,000 BTUs. A gallon of gasoline contains about 116,000 BTUs and conventional diesel fuel contains about 139,000 BTUs. Gallon for gallon, you need about 1.5 gallons of ethanol to get the same energy that is available in a gallon of gasoline, and almost two gallons of ethanol to get the same energy that is available in a gallon of diesel fuel. There is a reason that long haul over the road trucks are powered by diesel engines; they produce the most horsepower for the lowest cost. Diesel fuel is one of the easiest and safest liquid fuels to refine and process. Ethanol is so corrosive it can't be transported through existing pipelines. It has to be tankered in specially built trucks or rail cars. It can only be dispensed in specially designed pumps with specially designed hoses and rubber seals. And used above a concentration of about 10% in gasoline; it will void your new engine warranty. Diesel fuel is pumped out of an oil well. Ethanol is manufactured by consuming high energy content diesel fuel in the planting, harvesting, shipping, and storage of a valuable food crop, then diverting it into a low value fermentation process that consumes massive amounts of fresh water, pesticides and chemical fertilizer in order to produce a low energy content fuel. The net energy gains are pretty marginal. Corn ethanol may maintain a small niche in the energy sector, but it is vulnerable to a breakthrough in more promising and potentially more productive technologies.✧✧✧

Engines

Another factor in a true environmental comparison is the actual operating efficiency of the fuel and engine design. Diesel engines operate at about 45% efficiency, meaning that about half the energy content of the fuel is converted to power; the rest is lost as heat. Gasoline engines operate in the 30% percent range of efficiency. What about those gas-electric hybrids? A gas powered Toyota Corolla will get you about 38 mpg. A hybrid version will cost thousands of dollars more and maybe get you about 45 mpg, and come with some very expensive nickel-metal batteries, for which ore must be mined and processed, components manufactured, and then intensively recycled at the end of their useful life. And if you are ready to go all electric and recharge your car at night, you are more likely than not burning coal in some other state to get your electricity fix sent to you via high voltage transmission lines. The truth is, when matched with modern ultra low sulfur fuels, today's diesel engines are surprisingly clean and environmentally green.

Why so much discussion about oil and energy in a book about the bankruptcy of the American economy? Because you need wealth to pay off debt, and for most of us, you still need energy to create wealth. Ask India how they feel about being told to curb carbon emissions just as their economy is finally producing a real middle class and bringing millions of people out of poverty.

So what can we do about climate change? We can start with technological triage. It will be quite a few years before we can even begin to replace fossil fuels with alternative fuels and new technology in a way that will make a real dent in the energy mix and reduce carbon emissions in any significant way. We could however, make substantial gains relatively quickly if we take a global perspective on energy and environmental impacts.

During the Presidential election contest of 2008 Republican vice presidential candidate Governor Sarah Palin championed the idea of a natural gas pipeline from Alaska all the way down to the lower 48 to exploit Alaska's vast gas reserves to bring clean burning natural gas to America while reducing our imports of foreign energy. This is a really bad idea. It would take billions of dollars and several years before a project of that scale could even begin to break ground, let alone actually get built. With the potential for rapid development of huge reserves of natural gas already available in the lower 48, the economic value of such a pipeline is pretty doubtful. The economic answer, as well as the environmental answer, is to develop Alaska's natural gas potential and export as much of it as possible to China in LNG tankers and displace the use of coal in China's economy.

This is what I mean by technological triage. The trade off would be an economic and environmental win-win scenario. Alaska would get an easy path to develop its natural resources in a way that would pay not only big financial dividends but directly contribute to the reduction in China's output of carbon emissions. I am pretty sure the science and economics would hold up. I am not sure the environmental lobby would be intellectually honest enough to let it happen. Would you be willing to trade a few acres of artic tundra for a carbon emissions reduction treaty with China? I would make that deal in a heart beat.

The point is, there is an enormous amount of progress that can be made in making the use of fossil fuels less carbon intensive without chasing after marginal technologies that are not ready for commercialization. There is plenty of low hanging fruit out there. Let's get at that stuff first. And yes, it is true you will get better gas mileage if your tires are properly inflated. So go and check them again.

Health Reform

America has a health problem, but it is not a health *care* problem. We have great healthcare in this country, on the cutting edge of innovation. We have the best technology and the best research in the world. So what is the problem again? The problem is not healthcare. The problem is health behavior, and health financing. We want healthcare, as long as someone else pays for it. We are actually pretty good at healthcare; we just suck at being healthy. We sit around all day. We drink too much, smoke too much, and we move too little. And we eat too much. We're just too fat. Obesity is out of control. According to the Centers for Disease Control and Prevention, about one in three of us are too fat. The inventory of chronic diseases caused by obesity that we manage with our health care dollars reads like a Frankenstein's monster of misery and woe:

Obesity Related Chronic Illness

- Coronary heart disease
- Type 2 diabetes
- Cancers (endometrial, breast, and colon)
- Hypertension (high blood pressure)
- Dyslipidemia (for example, high total cholesterol or high levels of triglycerides)
- Stroke
- Liver and Gallbladder disease
- Sleep apnea and respiratory problems
- Osteoarthritis (a degeneration of cartilage and its underlying bone within a joint)
- Gynecological problems (abnormal menses, infertility)

And let's not forget the big one: Erectile Dysfunction. The reason you have hyper-tension, coronary disease, diabetes, sleep apnea, need a knee joint replacement and can't get it up is because you are *too fat*. But don't worry; we can give you a pill for that too. Do you think that your smoking, drinking, lack of physical activity and dietary habits are a private matter of personal concern? Is your inner libertarian ready to stand up and fight for your right to express your rotundity? Do you think healthcare is a "right?" And that after walking around with an extra 60 pounds on your knee joints for 65 years that Medicare should buy you a pair of new ones? And pay for all of your complications from chronic diabetes after a life time diet of sugary snacks as well? Consider this:

Less than 15% of the cost of medical care for chronic lifestyle diseases as a consequence of being overweight or obese is borne by the patient. 85% of the cost is shifted to society as whole, either through private insurance, which raises the cost to everyone, or to Medicare. Almost half the cost of obesity related healthcare is borne by Medicaid and Medicare alone.

Lest you conclude I am being mean to old fat people, the problem is getting worse and not better in our kids. Since 1980 childhood obesity in the 12-19 year old age group has more than tripled from 5% to almost 18%. Pre-teen children are showing signs of cardiovascular disease that you wouldn't expect to see until decades later in life.

Our country is in the midst of a terrible health crisis that will take two generations to solve, but it is not a health *care* crisis. The crisis is not in the quality or quantity of care that is provided. The problem is health behavior, (our lifestyles mostly) and health financing. How do we pay for all that chronic care?

Financing is the problem. Expressed less delicately, the problem is too many people are surviving. The dirty little secret in health care financing is that technology is getting better and people are living longer than expected. Ouch. It sounds cold, but it is an inconvenient truth. As our ability to cope with what in the past would have been fatal diagnoses are becoming more manageable chronic conditions, it means that more people will use more healthcare dollars for a longer period of their lives than the system was designed for. And most of the cost will be shifted to someone else. But that is what insurance is supposed to do, right? Well, maybe.

In a private insurance market, such as for auto insurance, the government mandates that as a condition to driving upon the public roadways I have a valid license to drive a car and buy insurance to protect other people in case I screw up. The government gets to evaluate my driving skills and monitor my behavior, and can take away my license if my behavior makes me a danger to the public. The insurance company also gets to monitor and evaluate my behavior, and adjust the price of my insurance according to the risks associated with my behavior. If I go too fast, my insurance rate goes up. If I hit another vehicle, my insurance rate goes up. If I go too fast and hit another vehicle while intoxicated, the government will cancel my license and my insurance company will drop my coverage.

There is a direct consequence between my behavior and the price of my privilege, (not right) to occupy the public roadways with my car. Insurance is a zero sum game. Everybody in the risk pool pays for everyone else's accidents. The best I can do is try to change my behavior to acceptable standards and get into the lowest priced risk pool. And by the way, if I crash my car, the insurance company will decide whether or not to fix it based on the remaining value of the car.

Human life is not analogous to car insurance, I get that. It is just an illustration. But it is also true that the pricing mechanism for health care finance (insurance) is completely dysfunctional.

A for-profit health care system is fraught with moral dangers and ethical dilemmas: how much care to provide, who pays, who gets to decide, denial of coverage for pre-existing conditions, denial of promising treatments that are too expensive, withholding of patents for orphan drugs, to name just a few. But these dilemmas do not magically disappear under a non-profit single payer healthcare system. The same questions remain; we just call them by different names.

The debate is full of hypocrisy and delusions on both sides to obscure some true facts about healthcare. The truth is you cannot make a single payer healthcare system work without mandating participation and coverage. You have to force young and healthy low risk people to buy health insurance and put them into the risk pool with older and less healthy people. You have to transfer the cost of being old and sick onto the young and healthy.

You will also have to ration healthcare. This we already do. In the private market rationing is done by cost. If you can pay, you can play. Under a public healthcare system rationing is accomplished through limiting access. Uncontrolled healthcare costs are bankrupting us.

In the private insurance market, an insurance company will ask detailed and intrusive questions about my health history, my family history, my most intimate and personal behavior choices, what I eat, what I drink, where I live, who I live with, and what type of work I do. And if I want the coverage, I will answer the questions.

Under a public health care system the same questions that seem totally rational and benign, useful for pricing me into the appropriate for-profit risk pool, the essence of a free market system, suddenly become an ominous foreboding of government social engineering. Suddenly the exact same process gets derided as nanny-care restrictions on my personal liberty to destroy my lungs with cigarettes, and drown my liver in alcohol.

Public or private, the facts are undeniable. We want more healthcare than we are willing to pay for. In real life, the value of spending several thousands of dollars on a knee replacement for an 80 year old great grandfather is a legitimate question, unless he happens to be your 80 year old great grandfather.

I don't have an answer for this one. In 1965 when the Medicare system was put into place to provide health insurance coverage for retirees, I seriously doubt the cost accountants at the Congressional Budget Office ever envisioned titanium rocket ship parts would be used to replace worn out joints and nuclear particle accelerators would be used for diagnostic and therapeutic care. Medicare is going to go bankrupt not because of a lack of resources, but because recent advances in medical technology has outstripped our capacity to pay for it. So do your part. Lose weight, quit smoking, eat right and exercise. It might even save you some money. At the very least, change your attitude. It is not the government's job to take care of you. You are supposed to do that yourself.

Ultimately, the only real solution to the crisis in health finance is to put *more* of the health burden on the consumer, not less. Cost shifting in healthcare has been proven a complete disaster. If 85% of the medical costs associated with obesity were paid by the individual instead of being socialized, you would see a lot more people at the gym.

Personal responsibility and healthcare is one of those uncomfortable topics no one likes to talk about. But peace of mind has an economic value. The truth is that insurance only works if there are enough people in the risk pool who never use the insurance for which they have paid to pay for those that do. There are only two ways to do this. Force more people to buy health insurance to spread out the cost across a larger risk pool, and then also charge premiums according to an individualized standard set of risk factors. The pure economic solution is to mandate health insurance coverage and privatize the cost. I am not suggesting we all fly off the trapeze without a safety net. I am saying that it is reasonable to charge higher premiums and higher deductibles for those ailments that are closely related to behavioral choices. I am not suggesting government intrusion or coercion into everyone's dietary and lifestyle choices; but choices have consequences, and these should be reflected in the cost of my healthcare plan. Is this a socially acceptable solution? I doubt we could be that honest with ourselves.

How would a publicly mandated-privatized burden healthcare system work? First of all, the employer based healthcare system should be scrapped completely. It is a complete failure and puts American companies and American workers at a competitive disadvantage to the rest of the world. It is not your employer's job to take care of you either. You want Cadillac health care? Be prepared to pay for it on your own dime.

Healthcare insurance should be an individualized mandated burden paid for by the employee, not the employer. If you believe that access to health care is an individual "right" then you should be intellectually honest enough to recognize that the cost of enforcing that "right" should also belong to the individual. We have to be willing to make the connection between personal "right" and personal responsibility. The truth is simple. People respect what they pay for. What about the working poor and the unemployed? What about the sick, the elderly and disabled? I am not heartless, but everyone should pay *something*.

One of the great mantras for universal heathcare coverage is that costs will go down because early preventative care will result in a reduction in very expensive acute care delivered in emergency room settings. I doubt this logic holds. It is much more likely that mandated health care premiums paid for even by the lowest wage earner would have a much more powerful incentive to get a check up, on the theory that, if I have to pay for it, I might as well take advantage of it.

A more straight forward strategy for national economic survival would be to simply raise the aged based eligibility for Medicare coverage from age 65 to age 75. This would never happen of course. The AARP would crucify any politician with the temerity to propose such a radical change, so in the end, the system will stumble along and collapse into bankruptcy one way or the other, or face radical premium increases and radical rationing of care.

It is time to renegotiate our social contracts. We can do so in an orderly manner, and provide for our most vulnerable citizens, as we should. Then we should also recognize that Medicare was never designed to sustain the technological intensity that modern health science is capable of delivering in the most desperate medical circumstances. Or we can let the entire system collapse into default and let it take the economy down with it.

Innovate

The real wild card in the rebuilding of American prosperity is innovation. The unknown X-Factor, the next undiscovered thing, the next "It" that changes the game; this is where we travel off the map.

There is no way of knowing from where the next big thing will come. It could be out there right now, some break through in organic chemistry that makes growing algae for bio-diesel fuel ridiculously cheap and easy, or maybe it will come in high temperature super conductors that makes transmission of electrical power vastly more efficient than today.

Just today, at the time of this writing, a quick surf on the internet revealed the following innovative research being conducted by scientists at the University of Ohio: It may be entirely practicable to use urine from farm animals (and humans) as a source of hydrogen to power fuel cells on a commercial scale. Evidently, the chemistry is fairly straight forward.

It has long been known and often demonstrated in middle school science classes all across the country that you can extract hydrogen gas from water by running an electric current through it. Water is two hydrogen atoms bonded to an oxygen atom. Split the bond and the hydrogen gas is released. The problem is it takes a prohibitively expensive amount of electricity to get the hydrogen out this way, so it is not practical as an economic means of extracting hydrogen for use in a fuel cell.

Apparently, some scientists at the University of Ohio have observed that the hydrogen in the chemical compound called urea, which is a major component of urine, is made of four atoms of hydrogen bonded to two atoms of nitrogen. And guess what? Stick an electrode into a jar of urine and run a current through it and the process of electrolysis that releases the hydrogen gas is *33 times* more efficient. Soon, we may all pee into the gas tanks of our new fuel cell driven cars to make them go. The theoretical limit appears to be a car that can go 90 miles on a gallon of pee. Now that is innovation!

I am sure there are some technical constraints along the way before we see the new Ford pee-150, but think of the possibility of solving a huge waste processing problem at commercial scale feed lots by collecting all of the liquid waste and siphoning off the hydrogen gas for power production. It would probably displace a lot of those nasty carbon emitting fossil fuels too. Is this it? Is this the next big thing?

Of course, I have no idea what the next big thing will be. I do know it will probably cost a lot of money and take a lot time and a lot of research to commercialize it and bring it up to a scale that will actually have an impact on the productive capacity of the economy in a meaningful way.

But I do know this. America has enjoyed the strategic high ground in innovation and invention for more than two centuries. We have been blessed with the most efficient factories, the most innovative entrepreneurs and the most productive universities in the world, and we absolutely must seize a new strategic high ground for economic survival in the new century. We must boost innovation along, and incentivize universities and entrepreneurs to spend more money and make more investments in research and development to bring more new ideas to market more quickly.

We should declare a 10 year tax holiday at the United States Patent Office. For a special limited time offer, let's turn loose the potential of the young, the ambitious, the creative and the inventive. Let's offer a 10 year tax holiday on new processes and new inventions submitted for patent. Open the tax free window for three years, maybe even five years, and put American innovation on sale!

We should tell our scientists, researchers and inventors: bring in your new technology and your new exotic material! Bring it in for patent within the three year tax free window, and for the next ten years pay zero capital gains taxes and zero income taxes on the first sale or royalties paid for licensing your new technology.

This would start a new gold rush in research and development that scientists, inventors, and entrepreneurs would clamor to get in on. It would create a boom in investment and creativity that would far surpass a government funded "stimulus" package. The cost in new government spending? Zero. The transformative effects upon the productive capacity of the U.S. economy? Priceless.

We know from our own experience that every national crisis that demanded using our strategic reserve of debt capacity to ensure our survival was paid down once the crisis had passed by the productive capacity of a vastly expanded national economy. Today, we owe so much money to so many people, and our capacity to borrow more in a national emergency is now so limited, we should be putting our innovators and scientists on a war time footing. We should be scrambling like crazy to make it easy for people to get rich on good ideas.

The right to profit from one's inventiveness is deeply rooted in the American experience. Intellectual property rights, the right to patent, to own and control the use of one's inventions is the only individual property right that is specifically and explicitly mentioned in the body of the Constitution of the United States.

The language of the U.S. Constitution addresses the form, function, operation, divisions of power, and limitations on government authority. In only one place in the Constitution is a specific private property right actually mentioned in specific detail; Article One, Section 8, Clause 8 authorizes Congress to secure to inventors exclusive rights to their discoveries.

Immediately after forming the new government the U.S. Congress exercised this grant of Federal Power and passed the Patent Act of 1790. There is no law higher in the land. Even the Supreme Court can not overturn the Patent Act. It is incorporated into the very fabric of the Republic. That is how strongly the framers of our constitutional democracy felt about the right to profit from creating something new. It is part of the very essence of what it means to be an American, to own the fruits of your own labor, to reward creativity, promote invention, and celebrate innovation. And it is still the key that will restore and expand American prosperity.

Just Do It
Re -invent Education and Work

Geeks rule, nerds are cool, and dorks are hot. Not only do we have to kick start a new industrial revolution by rewarding and promoting invention, we must re-think and re-invent education and work. There was a time when a college education was a pathway to a middle class standard of living. Today, for many it will be a pathway to frustration, indebtedness, disappointment and despair.

Democratization of higher education has been a great boon to the country. Greater access to higher education, especially for women and minorities, has achieved great advances in social justice in the past two generations. It has yielded marvelous triumphs in achievement that only would be possible within the context of the American Experience. These are rightfully celebrated.

But it should also be noted that education is an industry like any other, and like any other industry, education needs profits to survive. In the great public research universities across the land the lexicon might be grants instead of profits, but the effect is the same. Institutions of learning survive by extracting wealth from their customers, and colleges and universities have become really, really good at it. Unfortunately, the holy grail of a liberal arts education is rapidly becoming a prohibitively expensive proposition for much of the middle class.

After World War II the GI Bill democratized access to higher education and paved the way for millions of men and women who came of age in the midst of depression and global war to a middle class standard of living for the first time in their lives. It was a model of success for an entire generation of families to produce their first generation of college educated children, my father included.

The goal of creating opportunity in education as a pathway to success and prosperity is a noble and cherished aspiration, and is rightly championed. But today, the ideal of a college education as a guarantee to middle class prosperity that is being promoted by the student loan-shark industry is a denial of economic reality. And a popular culture that celebrates college life as a four year right of passage of self inflicted brain damage and promiscuous sex certainly doesn't help. I got news for you guys at the party schools. While you were out stumbling around with your boxer shorts on your head, the geeks and nerds at the technical colleges in China, India, and yes, even the United States were busy inventing their future and most decidedly impacting yours. So, party on dude.

The truth is, sacrificing to get an education used to be worth something. Today, we are impoverishing entire families, two and sometimes three generations, for the privilege of paying Cadillac prices for a Chevrolet product. Students at mid-tier institutions are racking up student loan debts the size of house mortgages to graduate with degrees that qualify them for little else than the barista job at the local Starbucks.

Don't get me wrong, I am an absolute believer in the intrinsic value of a liberal arts education and the power of a mind set free, but when we convince families of slightly above average children to commit themselves to the burden of years of massive indebtedness with little hope of ever paying it off; that is crime against humanity.

We are turning a generation of kids raised on self-esteem and instant gratification into share croppers, modern indentured servants, who will suffer for years to sustain the perks and privileges of mediocre professors at mediocre institutions, who remain committed to an obsolete conception of the process of education and learning.

I admit it. I am an elitist. The best and the brightest should get into the best schools. But I do not believe in elitism. We should always be striving to level the playing field, break down barriers to access while demanding achievement and fostering a meritocracy whereever we can. But it is also dangerous to society that if you are not a graduate of one of the top ten law schools in the country and graduate in the top 10% of your class; your prospects in the legal profession are radically diminished from the day you receive your diploma. Attorneys and law firms are an incestuous and condescending priesthood, and guard their privileges jealously.

One of the reasons there are so many law schools in the United States is that law schools are incredibly easy to run and enjoy monopoly profits that in any other industry would be closely scrutinized as violating anti-trust laws. Very few states have an alternative path to academic qualification to sit for their state's bar exam that doesn't involve an antiquated formula for accreditation that still counts the numbers of volumes in the library and hours of time spent in class, despite the fact that no one does legal research in an actual library anymore, (it is all done over the internet now, where else?) And most students today spend way more time in chat rooms and virtual study groups than they do actually sitting in a classroom. Fortunately for me, California allows on line and virtual classes to count for academic credit, and there are legitimate virtual law schools out there.

A law degree from a private law school now approaches $200,000 in tuition, books, fees, room and board. It is getting really hard to make enough money as a young attorney to pay off those student loans when LegalZoom is on television promoting do-it-yourself legal services for $69. I completed my law degree completely on line for about $30,000 in total fees, and passed the California Bar Exam, one of the most difficult in the country, on the first try.

The problem of over selling, over promising, and over charging for a mediocre product produced by an archaic educational model extends far beyond undergraduate and professional schools. Some of the private vocational and trade schools are just as problematic. For a mere $50,000 in tuition and fees, you too can become a Cordon Blue Chef, trained in the culinary arts for an exciting career in the hospitality industry... earning about $12.50 per hour.

What is the answer? A vastly expanded two year community college system throughout the country; Professor John McWhorter at Columbia University states the answer:

"One of the most pernicious myths ... is that you have to have four years of college at high tuition to have a decent existence. But who installed your cable TV? Was it a ... guy with a degree from Northwestern? Who fixed your air conditioner or your refrigerator when it last broke? How many sound technicians, building inspectors or mechanics fondly recount their days at UCLA? The path to many of these jobs and others is community college. You spend a couple of years getting a certificate or an Associate in Arts degree. It's not expensive and loans are not hard to get.... It's well known that plumbers make a thoroughly decent living. Do you think air conditioner repairmen are living hand to mouth?"

Is that too blue collar for you? Where do you think all those "green economy" jobs are going to be? They are going to go the trained technicians who know how to service a fuel cell, install a solar system, and disassemble the transmission box on a wind turbine, and they will get paid handsomely for doing it. Man does not live by bread alone, but you can't eat your diploma either. It may take a little longer, but the economic earthquake that destroyed General Motors and union labor will inevitably crumble even the most hallowed halls of academia if the delivery of educational services does not keep pace with the reality of the times. The ivory tower of academia is going to be replaced by a broader, flatter, and ultimately more egalitarian system of open access to education that will be available on demand, available to anyone, anywhere, at anytime, and that should be a good thing. And it will ultimately lead to a more productive and prosperous future.

✧✧✧ **CONCLUSION** ✧✧✧

✧✧✧

Where Did All the Money Go?

The Greatest Generation won the prosperity of our times by sacrificing its blood and treasure, and spent 35 years from the end of World War II until 1981 paying down the debts left over from a decade of economic depression and five years of global war. The Boomer Generation that followed has enjoyed the greatest legacy of wealth and prosperity ever bestowed from one generation to the next, and then they kept the party going as long as they could by delaying the day of reckoning and racking up the bill. This should not be the legacy we leave our children. Our children should not be the first Generation of Americans to have fewer opportunities for prosperity and success than their parents. They do not deserve to be the Busted Generation.

The question is: Where did all the money go? We are a fabulously wealthy society with the greatest potential to adapt, innovate and succeed, even in a new world of hyper competitive global markets. But the capacity for prosperity and the achievement of prosperity require both the right tools and right state of mind. The truth is there is no shortage of money out there. China's new middle class society alone is adding more than a trillion dollars a year to the global savings pool. This is money that should be available for investment in new technologies and new industries, but instead is being locked up in U.S. government bonds. All that money is being sucked away from investment in productive capacity, and is being used instead to finance our deficits in trade and government spending. We are spending it faster than the Chinese can save it.

We need to rebalance our economy, rebalance our trade relationship with China and the rest of the world, and spend less on consumption. We must reverse the crushing transfer of income from younger Americans to older Americans through an unsustainable system of entitlements. I am sorry, all you baby boomers out there, but your children simply cannot afford to keep you in the lifestyle to which you have become accustomed.

Paying Taxes Makes You Rich

Nothing is more sacred to economists and free market believers than the idea that taxes are a drag on economic growth and distort the incentives of the market place to diminish overall productivity in the economy. At punitive levels of taxation, this is a fair position to take. On the other hand, there is ample evidence in real world observations to suggest that levels of taxation that are *too low* also diminish productivity in the economy.

"No New Taxes!" as a battle cry makes great political theater, but it is just lousy economics. There are three pretty good measures of determining the wealth creating potential of a society. These are (1) private property (2) innovation and (3) taxation. Just like the proverbial three legged stool, the success of each depends upon the support of the other two. Private property and innovation are pretty intuitive. Taxation is not, but it is true. Paying taxes makes you rich. (Pause for incredulous laughter....) I am quite serious.

Taxation serves a valuable public purpose. There are a few fundamental bargains we make in order to enjoy the benefits of a well ordered and peaceful society, and one of them is a guarantee of private property rights. You get to keep your stuff. If someone takes your stuff, the government will spend its own money to get the guy that took your stuff. This applies to conduct by the government too. The constitutional guarantee of private property rights means the government can't take your stuff either. And for this guarantee of both enforcement and restraint by the government, we have the privilege of paying taxes.

Another one is the protection of inventions. Make something new and useful, and the government will protect your right to keep anyone from copying your idea without your permission. We call these patents, trademarks, and copyrights. The right to own what you invent is explicitly written directly into the Constitution of the United States. In fact, once you get past the Declaration of Independence and the right to life, liberty, and the pursuit of happiness, almost everything that comes after, including the entire US Constitution is about the creation and protection of private property rights.

In exchange for these benefits, The U.S. Constitution also gives the government the right to levy taxes to raise money to pay for the things you need to ensure the protection of private property rights; things like police and fire protection, defense from foreign invaders, etc., pretty important stuff like that. Perhaps the only thing as deeply rooted in the language of the Constitution as the protection of privacy and property rights is the power of the government to tax. How deep and vast is the power to tax? In every instance, those with the temerity to challenge the government's constitutional power to tax have been swept aside by the courts.

Whenever the Supreme Court has examined a challenge to the constitutionality of the congressional power to levy taxes it made definitive rulings: A tax is constitutional if (1) it is intended to raise money, or (2) actually raises money. Basically, the courts have said that the government has almost unlimited power to levy taxes, and it is not the courts job to decide how much taxation is too much. The power of the ballot box is only real restraint upon the government's power to levy taxes. At some point, people get angry enough about their taxes to throw the bums out and start over. Taxation and spending are at the heart of every political debate.

But the ability to levy taxes actually does serve an important wealth building function. Without a functioning level of taxation to protect private property, any incentive to invent or produce, or invest in the future would disappear. Rich societies have functioning governments that are funded by taxes, poor societies do not. And in failed states where government hardly exists at all, taxation is replaced by criminal extortion, intimidation, rape, and murder.

A simple illustration of how the power to levy taxes can increase wealth building potential is the construction of a bridge over a treacherous expanse of water separating two markets. San Francisco Bay is a perfect example.

The first technically feasible proposal for a bridge to span San Francisco Bay and relieve the bottleneck of ferry traffic across the channel dates to around 1916, but construction of the bridge did not become economically feasible until a 1928 Act of the California Legislature created the Golden Gate Bridge and Highway District to finance the design and construction of the bridge. In 1930, having been unable to raise the funds privately, supporters of the bridge project lobbied for a referendum to approve construction bonds to pay for the $35 million dollar project. In 1932, backed by the full faith and credit of the taxpayers of the affected counties, Amadeo Giannini, founder of Bank of America, bought the entire bond issue. The taxpayers had committed themselves to pay for the bridge.

Construction of the bridge began in 1933 during the darkest year of the depression when the unemployment rate was over 25%. 83,000 tons of steel needed for the bridge was manufactured in New Jersey, Pennsylvania and Maryland, and shipped through the Panama Canal to the construction site. In 1933 alone, the bridge project consumed 6% of the steel output of the entire country. Just one of the bridge piers built to support the weight of the suspension towers used more concrete than the entire Empire State Building. The bridge was completed in 1937, and came in $1.7 million dollars under budget.

What about those taxpayers who had pledged their guarantee of the construction bonds? The last of the construction bonds was paid off in 1971, including $39 million dollars in interest paid entirely from bridge tolls. The tax payers never paid a nickel. Just the power of a public guarantee of repayment alone was enough to make the bridge financially possible. Now that's an economic stimulus project anyone can love.

Today, more than 250,000 vehicles cross the bridge every day, and every four years, the time it took to originally build it, more money is spent on maintenance than it took to construct in the first place. Sometimes you don't even need the taxpayer's money to stimulate the economy. The power of a public guarantee alone through the commitment of the levy can be enough to make the impossible possible.

But there is a catch. It doesn't work if the tax is just a transfer payment. Taxes that only serve to transfer money from one group of society to another don't count. There is a huge difference. It only works if you are pledging the full faith and credit of the taxpayer as a guarantor to something that increases the productive capacity of the economy and becomes a useful economic asset on its own. The full faith and credit of the taxpayers made the financing and construction of the Golden Gate bridge a reality, but the bridge actually paid for itself, and San Francisco is all the more wealthy because of it, as well as a few famous song writers too.

The lesson is, don't let yourself be sucked into a debate over government borrowing and spending, and how we are impoverishing our children with a crushing debt, unless you examine the question for what *purpose* are we borrowing money and will the debt, or even just the guarantee of a debt, add any *productive capacity* to the economy. A debt incurred that creates its own self amortizing revenue base is not a burden on future generations. It is an investment to build upon. In 1933 the $35 million dollars it took to build the golden gate bridge was *a lot* of money. The estimated cost to build the bridge today: Over $1.2 *billion* dollars.

Perhaps a better question would be: Would we even build it today? How many years of environmental studies, lawsuits, and regulatory delays would it take before construction would even begin? In 1942 the Pentagon, the world's largest office building, was completed in 16 months, even with the requirement it use a minimum of steel, which was in short supply for war production. The Pentagon is so large the US postal service assigned six different zip codes to the building just to route the mail. Today, we still have nothing to replace the twin towers at the World Trade Center almost ten years after September 11, 2001. I think we should get on with it.

Thomas Friedman in his recent book described America as a "Banana Republic", meaning: "Build Absolutely Nothing Anywhere Near Anyone". There is no entitlement to prosperity. We have to go out and earn it, and yes, we will even have to pay taxes for the privilege. Prosperity and taxes are not mutually exclusive. But we must have the political will for both.   For the sake of the next generation that is staring national bankruptcy in the face, I hope we can find the will to build great things, invest in a more productive economy, and then tax ourselves appropriately to ensure the prosperity and the liberty for another generation of Americans.

✧✧✧

Epilogue

Since finishing this book in the spring of 2010, here are just some of the recent events that are currently in the news. We have our work cut out for us.

Oil- An offshore drilling rig operated by BP exploded and sank, and is still spilling 200,000 gallons of oil a day into the Gulf of Mexico.

Stock Prices- stock prices suddenly and mysteriously collapsed in a total free fall. In a matter of minutes the Dow dropped over 1,000 points before recovering. Regulators are still mystified as to how electronic trading programs "took over' the stock market before human intervention could stop the destruction.

Healthcare - Analysts and the OMB have uncovered another $115 Billion in costs buried in the healthcare bill.

Bailouts- The IMF imposed austerity measures on the Greek government to avoid a potentially crippling debt default. Angry public employees in Greece riot in the streets. The Euro is rescued with a trillion dollars in new public debt obligations.

Entitlements- The Social Security Administration Trustees report that the fund will go bankrupt years before the most recent projections due to drastic reduction in payroll tax receipts as a result in the loss of jobs and the lingering recession.

Unemployment- New unemployment claims drop, but the unemployment rate goes up to 9.9% as more people start looking for work.

Acknowledgements

I would like to acknowledge the following people for their help with this book.

Dr. Karl Egge
Chair of the Economics Department
Macalester College, Saint Paul MN

Mark Hewitt
Chairman and CEO
Northwoods Bank
Park Rapids MN

Lt. Col. George Eaton, (ret)
Command Historian, U.S. Army
Rock Island Arsenal
Davenport, IA

Ellis Jones, Rory Palm,
and Pam Norby, who laboriously corrected my lousy
punctuation, syntax, and grammar; any remaining mistakes are
mine, not theirs.

And, of course, Keiko, who has waited patiently through
several drafts and rewrites for me to actually get it finished,
and created the final design and layout of the book.

Any mistakes of fact are mine, and any opinions expressed in
the book should not be attributed to anyone but me. I have tried
to give proper attribution where it is due. I regret any omissions
where they exist.

Y

www.ingramcontent.com/pod-product-compliance
Lightning Source LLC
Chambersburg PA
CBHW062138280526
45788CB00001B/211